D0187978

The WORLD *on a* PLATE

This book complements a ten-part television series. During the course of filming I ate ants' eggs and armadillo, clambered over pyramids and gave a massage to a Japanese steer while being directed, encouraged and chaperoned by a large team who, like me, have lived, breathed – and often eaten – this series with devotion and enthusiasm. Any television series as broad in scope and execution as this one is a collaborative effort and the role of everyone on the team has been absolutely vital. I am very grateful to Peter Gillbe and Simon Andreae, his deputy at Optomen Television, who carefully shepherded the programmes from conception to broadcast. I am grateful, too, to Francois Le Bayon for all his help. Lesley Gardner, Adam Berman, Kate Fenhalls and Jane Atkinson made sure that we were all in the right places at the right times – a sometimes impossible-seeming job, carried out by them with unfailing good humour. Our researchers Brigitte Downey, Fiona Law, Kerry McKibbin, James Norton, Kate Scholefield and Nigel Paterson were graceful even under unusual amounts of pressure. Malcolm Clark, Martin O'Collins, Ron Johnston and Habie Schwarz directed the programmes with keenness and intelligence, and our superb team of film crews performed brilliantly under the most trying conditions. My thanks go to Stephen Foster, Steve Phillips, Phil James, Andrew Cross, Luke Cardiff, Richard Hill, Jason Russell, John Warwick, Robert Hill, Mark Hatch, Nick Plowright, Gerry Law, David Hall, Chris Openshaw, Andrew Thompson, Adrian Bell, Clive North, Steve Shearn, Ashley Mills and Elmer Postle – it was a pleasure to work with you all. It was also a pleasure to work again with Sheila Ableman and Charlotte Lochhead at BBC Books and with my assiduous editor Tessa Clark.

This book is dedicated to my two estimable daughters, who were not always sure why I was away but made every homecoming a dream.

LOYD GROSSMAN

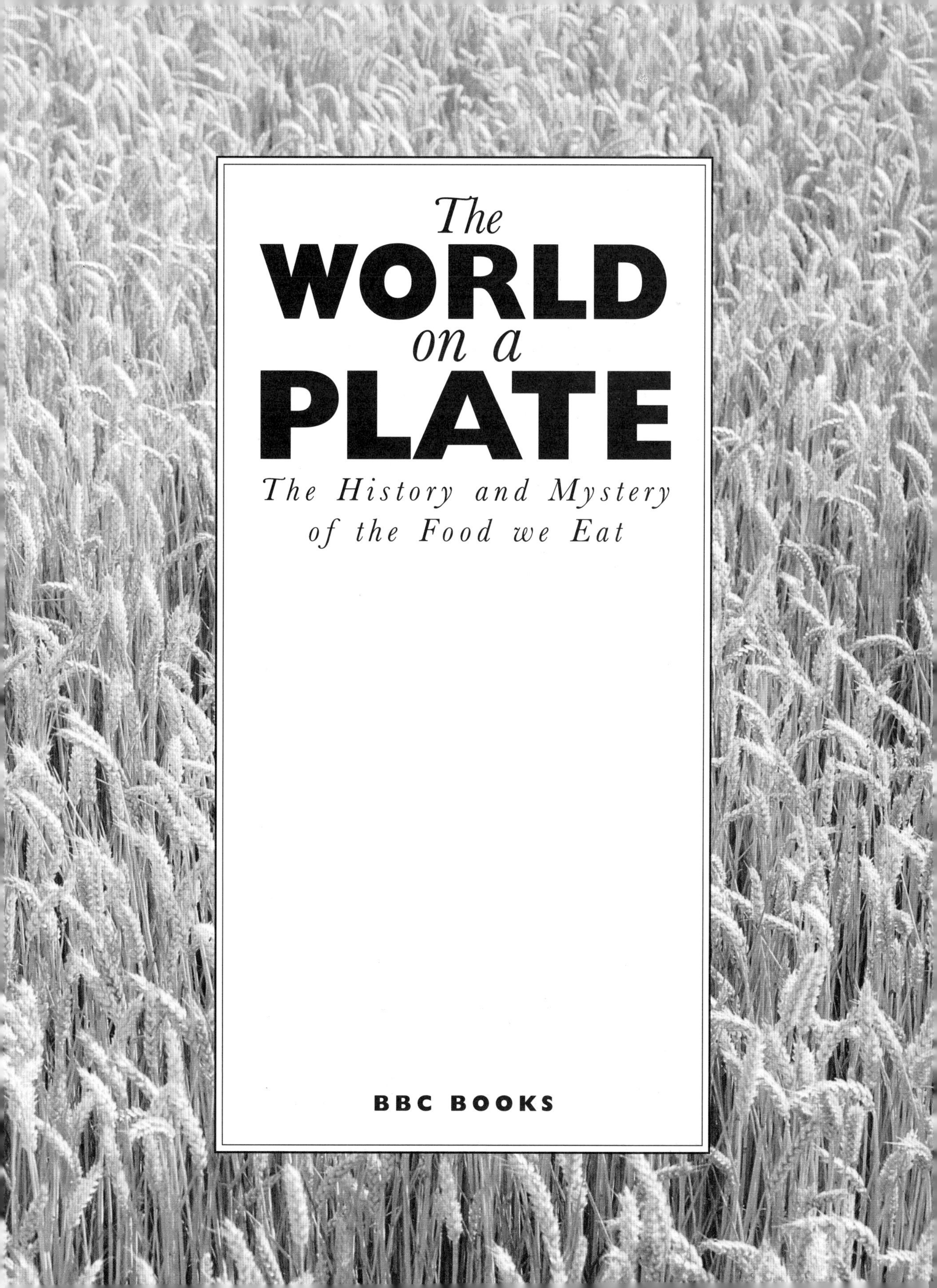

The WORLD on a PLATE

The History and Mystery of the Food we Eat

BBC BOOKS

This book is published to accompany
the television series entitled *The World on a Plate*
which was first broadcast in 1996.

Published by BBC Books
an imprint of BBC Worldwide Publishing,
BBC Worldwide Ltd, Woodlands, 80 Wood Lane,
London W12 0TT

First published 1996

ISBN 0 563 37097 1

DESIGNED BY HARRY GREEN

ILLUSTRATIONS BY ANNE ORMEROD

PICTURE CREDITS

BBC Books would like to thank the following for providing photographs and for permission to reproduce copyright material. While every effort has been made to trace and acknowledge all copyright holders, we would like to apologise should there have been any errors or omissions.

BBC/Justin Pumfrey 2/3 (bg); Anthony Blake Photo Library 14/15, 106/107; Bridgeman Art Library 34/35, 58/59; British Museum 31; J. Allan Cash 46/47; Colorific 82/83, 163; E.T. Archive 6, 23, 54/55; Robert Harding/Sharpshooters 182/183; Michael Holford 102/103; Hutchison Library 63, 214/215; Image Bank 150/151, 171, 202/203; Kobal Collection/Indo British Films/Columbia Pictures 90; Magnum Photos/Michael Nicholls 206; Pictor/Uniphoto 194/195; Rex Features/Sipa Press 198/199; Royal Geographical Society 86/87, 174/175; South American Pictures/Tony Morrison 130/131, 135, 138/139; Frank Spooner Pictures 158/159; Stock Boston/David Binder 74/75; Telegraph Colour Library 18/19, 78/79; Tony Stone Images 38/39, 66/67, 98/99, 115, 122, 178/179, 218/219; Tessa Traeger 110/111, 126/127, 186/187; © Valli-Summers 154/155; Victoria & Albert Museum 146/147; Zefa 42/43.

Set in Baskerville by Ace Filmsetting Ltd, Frome
Printed and bound in Great Britain by BPC Paulton Books Ltd, Bristol
Colour separations by Radstock Reproductions Ltd, Midsomer Norton
Jacket printed by Lawrence Allen Ltd, Weston-super-Mare

Contents

Prologue

Any history of food is not just about what we eat but about who eats it, when and why. Every culture is puzzled by other peoples' tastes. The English dismiss their historic enemies, the French, as 'Frogs', the French vilify the Anglo-Saxons as 'Rosbifs' and northern Italians sneer at the Tuscan fondness for vegetables with the epithet '*mangafagioles*' or 'bean-eaters'.

It is an attitude that was memorably summed up by Jean Anthelme Brillat-Savarin in the words: 'Tell me what you eat: I will tell you what you are.' A French bureaucrat of the Napoleonic era, he was also a political refugee, violinist, bon viveur and the author of *La Physiologie du Goût*, a book of gastronomic aphorisms, observations and philosophy published shortly before his death in 1825 and never subsequently out of print. Brillat-Savarin is immortalized by an egg and truffle flan, a syrup-soaked cake, a boned partridge, a thickened consommé flavoured with sorrel and various other dishes. His aphorism is perceptive and witty but the concept is not necessarily original.

The idea that the climate and topography of a land – and therefore the food it grows – moulds the character of its people was first formulated by Herodotus, the fifth century BC Greek traveller and writer who is celebrated as the father of history. He

The Italian artist Giuseppe Arcimboldo turned meticulous still lifes of flowers, fruit and vegetables into allegorical portraits. In 1591 he used the technique to portray his boss, the Holy Roman Emperor Rudolf II, as Vertumnus, the ancient Roman god of change.

looked at the most traumatic event in his lifetime, the dynamic expansion of the Persian Empire and its effects on the fledgling democracy of Greece, and wanted to understand why the Persians were so different from other peoples. At the end of his *History* he records how the victorious Persian army suggested to their king that they might abandon their mountainous homeland and live more comfortably in one of the countries they had conquered. Their ruler was unimpressed. 'Soft countries breed soft men,' he told his troops. 'It is not the property of any one soil to produce fine fruits and good soldiers too.' So Herodotus began to suggest the connection between character and consumption 2500 years ago. So, even more explicitly, did the Hindus in their sacred text the *Bhagavadgita*, 'The Song of the Lord'. In it Krishna, the amorous flute-playing divinity, observes that, 'Men who are pure like food which is pure, which gives health, mental strength and long life; which has taste, is soothing and nourishing and which makes glad the heart of man.' On the other hand, 'Men of darkness eat food which is stale and tasteless, which is rotten and left overnight, impure, unfit for holy offerings.' If we turn Krishna's digestive equation on its head we get good food = good men, bad food = bad men. You are what you eat.

Almost more importantly, you are also what you are seen to eat. After his heroic but nonetheless catastrophic defeat by the communist Vietminh at the battle of Dien Bien Phu in 1954, the French commander Brigadier General Christian de Castries requested a plate of chips for his first post-war meal. Would the fried potatoes help him to recover from the trauma of one of the greatest military defeats in French history? *Mais non.* The request for chips was no mere craving for comfort food. 'The general's request,' the semiologist Roland Barthes explains, 'was certainly not a vulgar materialistic reflex . . . The general understood well our national symbols; he knew that *les frites*, chips, are the alimentary sign of Frenchness.' The alimentary sign: what we eat is a symbol that identifies us as clearly as a French general's *kepi.*

Possibly the most intriguing examples of the symbolic power of food are the *tour de force* visual puns of the sixteenth-century mannerist painter Giuseppe Arcimboldo, who found favour at the court of the Habsburg emperors. In about 1563 he began a series of allegorical portraits in which faces were composed of fruit, vegetables, bits of trees, cooking utensils and occasionally books. Most striking of all his works is his painting of Rudolf II. Rudolf, it must be said, was a difficult man and a spectacularly unsuccessful emperor. He was highly intelligent and cultivated, a dabbler in astrology and alchemy and a notable art collector. But he was cursed with what one biographer described as 'an hereditary tendency towards insanity' and slipped deeper and deeper into reclusive manic depression until his own family replaced him as emperor with one of his younger brothers. Arcimboldo glorified and memorialized Rudolf as Vertumnus, the Roman god of change, in a portrait that depicts him with a turnip for an Adam's apple, pea pod eyebrows, apple cheeks, a pumpkin forehead, a celery moustache and artichoke shoulders. How funny, sweet and peculiar to paint your boss, the most powerful man in Europe, as a heap of fruit and vegetables. Either the doomed emperor had an unusually forgiving sense of humour or Arcimboldo's portrait flatters him as the lord of all he surveys, symbolically identifying him with the riches of the earth.

If food is identity, it is also memory. Christ instructed his followers to eat consecrated bread with the words, 'Do this in remembrance of me.' And the evocative power of what we eat was deftly summed up by the French writer Marcel Proust who used the taste of madeleines, little shell-shaped cakes, as a point of departure for his six-volume autobiographical novel *Remembrance of Things Past*: 'Once I had recognized the taste of the crumb of madeleine soaked in her decoction of lime flowers which my aunt used to give me,' Proust wrote, 'immediately the old grey house upon the street where her room was, rose up like the scenery of a theatre.' As Christ, Proust and millions of others recognized, to taste is to remember.

So food is remembrance, identity – and more. It is hardly surprising, then, that a definitive history of the subject will never be written. The subject is too vast and too loaded with cultural baggage and factual land mines ever to be satisfactorily squeezed between two covers. *The World on a Plate* does not even pretend to be complete, objective or indeed a work of original scholarship. It is instead an interpretative wander through some of the meandering paths of food history. And I am all too aware that it, like the television series which it accompanies and complements, approaches the subject from an American and European point of view. My hope is that after you have read it you will share my excitement and enthusiasm as you see how even our most ordinary foods are full of romance and adventure – monuments to human ingenuity and, sometimes, testaments to our wickedness and folly.

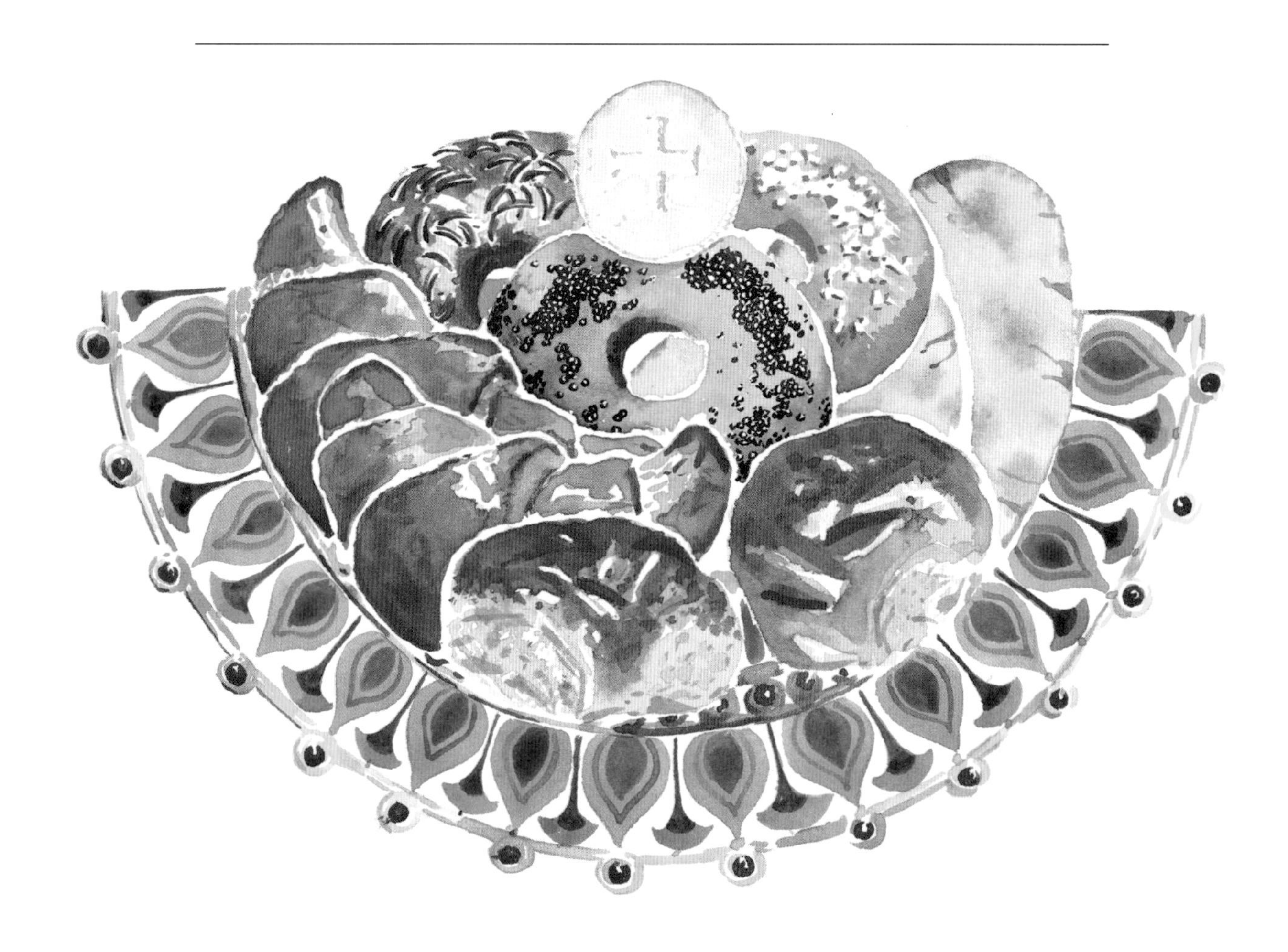

Bread of Heaven

I love bagels. These ring-shaped rolls are, as far as I know, unique in the world of baking because after the dough rises it is boiled briefly and then baked. The resulting concoction is hard on the outside, chewy on the inside – and, to my mind, delicious. Modern supermarkets sell slightly outlandish versions like cinnamon raisin ones and shoppers are advised to make pizzas out of bagels or slice them in half and fill them for sandwiches. When I was growing up in Boston, Massachusetts, in the 1950s you did not find them in supermarkets, you did not make pizzas out of them and you certainly did not turn them into ham sandwiches: bagels were a Jewish food that spread slowly from the crowded ghetto of lower East Side Manhattan in about 1900 to Jewish communities throughout the United States.

On Saturday nights we would go to the bakery and watch amazed as dough was transformed into bagels. Big, sweaty bakers in not very clean white T-shirts and aprons would form it into the familiar ring shapes. The rings were put into a huge vat of boiling water and would bob to the surface after a couple of minutes. They were then fished out of the water, placed on long-handled wooden paddles and thrust into enormously hot brick ovens. When the paddles emerged again the rings had become bagels. A hot bagel eaten almost straight off the baker's paddle was more delicious than any I have tasted before or since. (It is, of course, a *sine qua non* of food nostalgia that anything eaten in the past is incomparably better than what is eaten in the present.)

Watching the bagels being made was even more thrilling than eating them.

Eating was a straightforward sensory experience. Baking was magic, and the sweaty, ill-spoken bagel bakers were magicians. They had started with nothing special – flour – and transformed it into a delicacy. It is no wonder that John Lennon is supposed to have said that baking his first loaf of bread was the most creative thing he had ever done. Alas, no baker throughout recorded history has ever achieved his status. The familiarity of bread has meant, if not contempt, certainly indifference to the astonishing feat of the baker's midwifery: flour, yeast, water and fire give birth to bread or cakes or, in this case, bagels.

Bagels were first mentioned in Cracow, Poland, in the early seventeenth century, but their rise to more than local popularity began after the besieging Ottoman army was turned back from the gates of Vienna in 1683. The intervention of the king of Poland's cavalry was a decisive factor in the Turkish defeat and the hard little stirrup-shaped rolls were soon being sold in the streets of the city to commemorate the heroism of the Polish cavalry men. Steigbugel is German for 'stirrup' and bagel is a corruption.

Croissants also owe their fame to the siege of Vienna. They are part of a family of fancy baked goods which the french call *Viennoiserie* in honour of their birthplace. The struggle between the unwieldy Austrian Empire and the aggressive Turks for the control of central Europe was long and bloody. The attack on Vienna represented the high-water mark of Turkish intrusion into Europe and the Austrian victory marked the start of the long, slow decline of the Ottoman Empire. With the Turks defeated and Catholicism triumphant, it was time to celebrate. A Viennese baker who had been working in the small hours of the night was credited with being the first citizen to hear signs of the impending Turkish attack and was granted the honour of baking rolls in the shape of a crescent, the Ottoman symbol. The newly confident Viennese were able to symbolize their disdain for the Turks by blithely devouring a mouthful of the defeated enemy's badge. The croissant quickly spread across Europe as a tangible memento of a great event. And it was delicious too.

A close parallel to the croissant is the *hamantaschen*, a triangular pastry filled with a sweet poppy seed mixture. It is supposed to resemble the hat worn by

Haman, the wicked vizier whose plot to kill the Jews of Persia is told in the Old Testament book of Esther. During the festival of Purim, Jewish children greedily devour hamantaschen as a sweet reminder of the monstrous man after whom the pastries are named. So the croissant and the hamantaschen both add the insult of being eaten to the injury of defeat. And, like the bagel, they commemorate events. They are symbols.

Symbolism was on the menu when Jesus gathered his disciples together in a Jerusalem house on a Thursday evening sometime around the year 30 AD. The Last Supper may have been a ritual meal celebrating the beginning of the Jewish Passover; it unquestionably had the hallmarks of one. The disciples reclined – as was customary at formal banquets in the classical world – drank wine and sang. During the evening Christ, 'took bread and after giving thanks he broke it and gave it to them with the words, "This is my body".'

The disciples ate the bread and millions of devout Christians have imitated them ever since, believing to a lesser or greater extent that the consecrated wafer they eat is the body of Christ or, at the very least, a vivid reminder of their Saviour: you are what you eat. In the Coptic Church bread, rather than a wafer, is still used.

It is not for nothing that Christ used bread in the Last Supper. For millions of people, for thousands of years, it has been the staple *par excellence.* Our language reflects its central role as sustenance. We earn our daily bread. We call money 'bread' not just because we buy bread with it but also because the labourers who built the pyramids were partially paid in bread. To eat is to break bread. Our friends are our companions, those with whom we eat bread from the Latin *com* (with) and *panis* (bread). We know which side our bread is buttered on and when things go wrong it never falls but on its buttered side. We would

Overleaf: Bread has been a staple for thousands of years. Mezze – an array of small, savoury dishes served with bread – are reminiscent of ancient Greek meals where food was divided into two basic types: bread and everything else.

never stoop to take the bread out of another's mouth. When we eat our food is digested in our 'breadbasket' or stomach. While we console ourselves that man cannot live by bread alone we also praise what is marvellous as 'the greatest thing since sliced bread'.

But bread was not the first food. As we shall see, it arrived relatively late on the scene. Our earliest ancestors – and archaeology keeps pushing back the date of the first humans – probably dined out on a menu that was similar to that of their cousins the apes, subsisting on a diet of fruit, vegetables, ants, termites and, occasionally, each other. Sites of early human habitation provide us with numerous examples of flaked stones that could have been used as primitive cutting tools in the prehistoric kitchen. The remains of an elephant found with these stones at Olduvai Gorge in Africa show that our ancestors were butchering and presumably consuming big animals more than 1½ million years ago. Early men and women certainly ate plants but details of their diet remain a matter for speculation. Little is known except that it consisted of plants and meat and that at some stage a division of labour occurred after which men hunted and women gathered edible plants. The great step forward was the use of fire, which may have occurred about a million years ago. Fire enabled *Homo erectus* to widen his repertoire of food, particularly his meat diet. Ironically, the arrival of this bigger range of foodstuffs created medical problems: it seems likely that he sometimes suffered from overdoses of vitamin A brought on by eating too much cooked animal liver. Critically, fire changed the whole nature of mankind's relationship with food. It meant that the hitherto inedible could become the highly desirable. It also represented the first step in our increasingly shaky 'mastery' over nature.

For our story, however, the climacteric is what has become known as the agricultural revolution: the time roughly about 10 000 years ago when the systematic cultivation of previously wild plants and the domestication of animals made the growth of settled human communities possible. Like many profound revolutions in the course of history it did not happen at any one time in any one place. It occurred in a number of widely spread locations throughout the Old World, driven by the improving climate as the last ice age ended and by the increase in human populations. Wheat, barley, rice, millet and maize were developed from their wild progenitors, as were cattle, goats, sheep and pigs. Domestication and cultivation began to take some of the uncertainty out of human life.

Perhaps the densest concentration of early agriculture is found in the Fertile Crescent of the Middle East, a banana-shaped expanse of land that curves from the Persian Gulf up through what is now Iraq and Syria and down through Lebanon and Israel to the Egyptian border. Wild grasses with edible seed heads grew in abundance throughout this area, particularly on what some archaeologists call the 'hilly flanks of the Fertile Crescent'. Humans must have seen animals eating them and been inspired to try them too. The grain from these grasses was both highly nutritious and easy to store. The first steps towards the birth of agriculture may have been merely scattering the seeds to spread their growth. The biggest problem was that the seed heads had a propensity to burst as soon as they ripened so humans may have been on the look-out for varieties that held on to their heads longer. They were also probably able to observe that some were hardier than others. Fortunately the grasses crossbred in the wild. Early wheat varieties like emmer and einkorn (which still grow in their wild state in a few places in the Middle East) were domesticated into more easily harvested forms. Human hunger and empirical observation combined to create, however gradually, the rudiments of agriculture.

But why agriculture developed when it did is hotly debated. Certainly, in about 8000 BC the climate of the Middle East began to change and became

Overleaf: Ten thousand years ago the systematic cultivation of wild grasses like wheat was the great breakthrough that made settled human life and civilization possible. The agricultural revolution was concentrated in the Fertile Crescent of the Middle East before spreading throughout the ancient world. Today wheat is the most widely cultivated of the 80 000 varieties of edible plants that grow on earth.

drier. The once reliable rains lessened and human management was needed to ensure a supply of grain. But did our success at cultivating these formerly wild grasses lead to the growth of our first considerable settlements? Or did the development of larger settlements like the so-called Natufian villages in Palestine which were established as early as 10 000 BC compel humans to find a more efficient way of ensuring an adequate food supply? Who came first – the farmer or the villager? These questions are, at the moment, unanswerable. But we do know that the growth of settled human communities throughout the wheat-growing areas was explosive. Jericho and other early settlements are mere villages by modern standards – Catal Huyuk, the largest yet excavated, could fit comfortably within the gardens of Buckingham Palace – but in their own time they were considerable wonders. However, the settled life was not without its vicissitudes: crops failed, climates changed and house-building, charcoal-burning and grazing animals led to deforestation. Life, even in the new towns, was uncertain. Nevertheless agricultural settlements sprang up all over the Old World from the Kachi Plain of north-western India to north China and South-east Asia. The settled life encouraged the slow but steady growth of trade and the birth of political organization as villages grew into towns and cities. And it was all made possible by the management and domestication of wild plants and animals. Without the relative stability created by an agricultural system none of the things – ranging from football to art and warfare – that we distinguish as civilization could have developed their complex forms.

Food evolved alongside civilization. Wheat grain was mixed with water to make a variety of porridges and gruels before the great leap into baking and the invention of bread. All advances were based on ways of making wheat easier to digest and store. The grain itself consists of the embryo or wheatgerm, the endosperm or starchy portion which makes up its bulk and the tough outer husk and bran that protects it. So the first step must be to separate the relatively indigestible husk from the softer parts of the grain. (This process was often inefficient: mummies have terrible teeth because Egyptian grain was so coarse.) The remains then have to be milled into flour. For most of history this has been done between two stones although the familiar round millstones did not appear until Roman times. Bread is really a very sophisticated way of using the food potential of wheat: it is easy to handle, store, distribute and digest. Its convenience and portability make it a nutritional equivalent of the Sony Walkman. The first bread may well have come about by accident as some gruel dried in the fierce heat of the Middle Eastern sun: it would have been a dense, and to our taste rather unpalatable, cake but nonetheless a step forward. It was the Egyptians, who excelled in so many things, who developed what we would quite clearly recognize as bread.

Egypt was wheat-growing country. An island of water, the Nile was set in a sea of sand that stretched all the way from Asia to the Atlantic. Along the thin strip of fertile land on either side of the river, made rich by its annual flood, a powerful and complex civilization developed. The Egyptians enjoyed many of the things we do: dinner parties, pets, linen clothes for hot weather, comfortable furniture, strong beer. In many ways the gulf of some four millennia is not too wide. And because their everyday life is so familiar to us we are intrigued and often puzzled by the elaboration and rather morbid preoccupations of their spiritual life. The importance of wheat cultivation was enshrined in their religion. Wheat was the symbol of the god Osiris who brought agriculture to mankind and its life cycle was thought to echo the life of man. Grains of wheat were trodden into the ground in imitation of a human burial, rested there like a human soul in the underworld and then sprouted forth in the spring as a symbol of resurrection. Osiris was sometimes represented as white, sometimes as black and sometimes as green – the colour of new growing wheat and resurrection. Corn mummies, or small effigies of the god made from mud and grain, were often buried in Egyptian tombs: the sprouting of the seeds would ensure the afterlife of the deceased. Egyptian society was fuelled by bread – leavened bread, lighter and more delicious than its predecessor – and beer, twin products of wheat and the Nile.

Both rely on fermentation or the activity of yeast, a free-ranging and largely benevolent spore that brings about a number of biochemical changes in carbohydrates. The first leavened bread might have been created when yeast entered the breadmaking process from a nearby vat of fermenting beer, or perhaps merely floated on to a batch of wet dough and found it a convenient place in which to do its work. However it happened, the Egyptians made full use of this chemical reaction and leavened bread was soon an essential part of the settled life. We know that when Moses led the Jews out of their captivity in Egypt they left so quickly that their bread was baked before it had time to rise and that unleavened bread is still eaten on the commemorative feast of Passover. We also know that during their post-liberation period of wandering in the desert the Jews continued to eat unleavened bread as a sign of their nomadic status: leavening meant permanent settlement and was not reintroduced until they were led into the Promised Land.

In many ways the pyramids symbolize the significance of bread in Egyptian society. When the pharaohs of the Old Kingdom began building them in the third millennium BC – the greatest structures that had ever been built by man – they paid their workers partially in bread. After a pharaoh's death and entombment offerings of bread were brought to his pyramid each day. A recent academic foray into Egyptian baking by University of Chicago archaeologist Mark Lehner and retired doctor Edward Wood produced flower-pot-shaped loaves baked in clay moulds copied from Old Kingdom bas-reliefs. As reported by *National Geographic*, a thrilled Wood declared the bread was, 'sourdough bread the way it's meant to taste'. Delicious as that may sound, it is hard not to feel that a life of pyramid building, bread and beer was a monotonous recipe for the labourers of ancient Egypt. Bread still looms large in the Egyptian diet: *ayeesh*, the Arabic for 'bread', also means 'life'.

The Egyptian use of bread as a temple offering prefigures the moment

Christ was well aware of the evocative power of food. At the Last Supper (depicted here by the sixteenth-century Dutch painter Lucas van Leyden) he identified himself with bread, the staff of life in the Holy Land. Following his injunction to 'do this in remembrance of me' Christians still eat it in a ritual partaking of their saviour's body.

during the Last Supper when Christ gave bread to his disciples with the words, 'This is my body' – and also signals a move away from animal sacrifices. It is not too fanciful to see the miraculous transformation of dough into bread as evidence of divine power and its mysteries. In the Ukraine bread is regarded as a gift from God and stepping on it is sinful. If a piece is dropped it must be kissed after being picked up. Mundane in the extreme, bread remains divine.

Like the Egyptians, the Greeks used bread freely in religious ceremonies. Its high status is reflected in the importance of Demeter, mother goddess of the earth and grain goddess, in the Greek pantheon. The story of her daughter Persephone repeats many of the elements of the Egyptian Osiris myth. Persephone was abducted into the underworld by her uncle Hades. A furious Zeus ordered him to return her, but it was not possible: Persephone had eaten a pomegranate seed while she was in the underworld and bound herself to Hades. Zeus negotiated with his brother and Persephone was allowed to return to the world for half the year. According to the legend she remains below ground during winter waiting to rise again with the crops each spring. Bread was so significant a part of the Greek diet that, as Maguelonne Toussaint-Samat points out, foodstuffs were divided into bread and those that were not bread. (A similar division is practised by the Chinese who distinguish between rice and everything that is not rice.) A meal frequently consisted of a plate of flattish bread topped with vegetables, cheese, olives and meat or fish – not unlike a modern pizza. The Greeks developed a reasonably large repertoire of breads ranging from very dark ryes to fine white breads and ones flavoured with poppy seeds or enriched with milk. Their skill at baking is witnessed by the large number of Greek bakers who later set up shop in imperial Rome.

The Romans moved the technical goalposts of baking and developed superior methods of milling. They even used equipment like a mechanical device for kneading dough, attributed to the celebrated bakery Marcus Virgilius Eurysaces who became rich and prominent enough to rate an elaborate tomb decorated with bas-reliefs of bakery scenes. Like the Greeks, the Romans produced a huge variety of breads made not just from wheat but also from rye, barley, millet and even acorns in times of scarcity. They felt strongly, however, that coarse breads were for the coarser citizens and that fine, white, wheat breads were the proper ones for patricians. This idea influenced generations until health-consciousness made us re-evaluate the benefits of coarse, dark breads.

The Roman reliance on wheaten bread led to a prodigious international economic system based on the cultivation, shipping and storage of wheat. Egypt and North Africa were turned into the granary of the empire. Huge warehouses were built in Rome itself and the distribution of free bread and the strict regulation of wheat prices were used as instruments of political control. The Romans turned grain into an international commodity and it has remained one ever since, creating huge fortunes and also crises when prices were high and wheat was scarce. The pioneering work of Fernand Braudel reminds us that even during the flowering of Renaissance civilization, 'Grain was a preoccupation simply because it was always scarce: Mediterranean harvests usually verged on the inadequate . . . Wheat in the Mediterranean took up a great deal of room, requiring large areas for not very high yields, particularly since the same land could not be sown every year.' Grain flowed ceaselessly from often far-flung country farmers to city bakers. As a bishop in sixteenth-century Ragusa observed, 'In this city not a single grain of wheat is eaten which does not have to be fetched from five hundred miles away.'

Ironically, the Roman success in baking raised bread to a dietary pre-eminence that endured for centuries, condemning the mass of the European population to a dull diet that was overly reliant on bread. And one that was not only boring but extremely susceptible to the volatility of the grain supply. Bread riots became a feature of life in Europe. 'Let them eat cake', Marie Antoinette's flip and apocryphal remark to the bread-hungry Parisian mob, has resonances far beyond the narrow circumstances of the French Revolution. No wonder that some historians now feel that the hunted and gathered diet of humans before agriculture was richer, more varied and more appetizing than what was to follow. The assumption that the history of food is a story of progress is an assumption worth avoiding.

Sacred Staples and Taboos

CHAPTER 2

A quick check of my store cupboard reveals the following olive oils: one bottle of dark Greek oil from Kalamata, one bottle of chic and possibly over-priced oil from a Tuscan wine-maker in Italy, one big tin of light Provençal oil brought back from a holiday in the South of France, one bottle of oil from Portugal and one designer bottle of oil from Sonoma County, California. So, five different oils of different ancestry, all different to look at, taste, smell and pay for. The prices range from around £5 a litre for the Greek one to nearly £20 a litre for the Tuscan. My household uses quite a lot of olive oil – I guess somewhere between 1 and 2 litres (1¾ to 3½ pints) a week. We dress salads with it, make sauces with it, fry fish in it and use a dribble of it here and there to enrich the flavour of different dishes.

We like its taste and also feel that it is better for us than many other fats. Most people with even a minor interest in nutrition will be familiar with the studies that indicate that olive oil is rich in the family of fats known as monounsaturates and that these increase our levels of high-density lipoproteins which help to keep our cholesterol levels low leading to a longer and healthier life. Olive oil is also well endowed with other beneficial goodies like vitamin E and antioxidants. But this is not a chemistry lesson and notions, no matter how scientific, of what foods are good or bad for us change as quickly as Claudia Schiffer's hemline. But for the moment at least, a lot of people like me think that olive oil is good for you. More to the point, it tastes good too. So I do not think that my family's consumption of 50 to 55 litres (11 to 12 gallons) a year is either outrageous or out of the ordinary. Especially when you look at the folks who brought us democracy, philosophy *and* olive oil: the ancient Greeks.

The Greeks used olive oil as food and for lighting their lamps, perfuming themselves, bathing and on ritual occasions. Tangible evidence of the high regard in which they held it can be seen in any museum with a reasonable collection of antiquities. Among the clay pots there will be many varieties of *lekythoi* – containers for olive oil. Some plainly decorated ones were for use at the table. Others, usually white (the colour of death in ancient Greece), were more elaborately decorated and used for funeral libations. No wonder Lin Foxhall, a historian working at the University of Leicester, has worked out that an affluent Greek household of the fifth century BC would use anywhere from 200 to 330 litres (44 to 73 gallons) a year – a figure which is even more impressive when we remember that ancient Greece, even at its peak of sophistication, was a relatively poor country and that olive oil was even then a high ticket purchase.

The oil begins with the tree. Olive trees are handsome evergreens whose silvery green foliage lights up the landscape wherever they grow in the broad belt that stretches between the latitudes of 30° to 45° north: an area which extends from Morocco to the South of France and roughly defines the limits of Mediterranean civilization. Like other evergreen trees (the olive's cousins include lilac and privet) it is hardy and is able to withstand freezing temperatures – although not for long. Even in the benign conditions of the Mediterranean basin the weather could have tragic effects. In January 1709 heavy rains followed by a severe cold snap wiped out olive production in the South of France for a generation; and even though we continue to think of the Languedoc as one of the great olive areas of the world cultivation there has never recovered. But for most years, over most of the Mediterranean, the tree has been a sturdy and reliable producer which is why it spread so steadily from its home somewhere in modern Syria. Systematic olive cultivation may have begun in Crete, possibly as early as 5000 BC and by 1000 BC it had reached Spain. The trees like a dry climate and poorish soil and in the right surroundings (which the Mediterranean regions provide) they will go on producing for centuries. They are, however, very labour intensive. They require careful pruning and harvesting also calls for many hands: although the olives can be shaken, or indeed even beaten, from the trees the best oil comes from unbruised fruit that has been picked by hand at the correct stage of ripeness. A mature tree in good health produces 20 kilograms (44 pounds) of olives and will produce 4 litres (nearly a gallon) of olive oil. So when you look at a tree that has been assiduously nurtured and painstakingly harvested, picture four bottles of olive oil sitting on your kitchen shelves. My family alone would need the annual production of thirteen trees for our oil supply. No wonder it is expensive.

Two and a half thousand years ago the expense and general usefulness of olive oil all over the known world revolutionized Greek society. Indeed, it is perhaps not too fanciful to say that without the ancient world's love of olive oil, democracy might never have developed when and where it did. We owe much to the remarkable figure of Solon, traveller, poet, *de facto* economist and businessman who was appointed temporary dictator of Athens in the early part of the sixth century BC. The city-state and its hinterland Attica were convulsed by economic crisis. Small farmers were becoming heavily indebted, wealth was concentrated in fewer and fewer hands and the balance of trade (as we would call it now) was disastrous. Solon was a pragmatist. 'Laws,' he observed, 'are like spider's webs. If some poor weak creature come up against them, it is caught; but a bigger one can break through and get away.' He was determined not only that the 'poor weak creature' imprisoned or enslaved for debt should be freed, but also that the whole basis of the Attic economy should be rationalized. He realized that the thin, rocky soil made self-sufficiency a dangerous dream and encouraged the farmers to grow what they could grow well. Fortunately for the future prosperity of Athens, this meant olives and grapes and the resulting oil and wine could be exported and sold around the Mediterranean. Solon also encouraged the growth of trade and manufacturing in Athens, making it into a sort of ancient Hong Kong living on its wits and energy, by legislating that fathers must teach their sons a trade. Finally he changed the way government was run by replacing the old system whereby people's birth qualified them to participate in affairs of state with a property qualification that enabled the new class of prosperous manufacturers and traders to enter the government. Then, unlike almost any dictator before or since, he gave up office and returned to private life.

The society created by Solon's reforms and the olive tree's proclivity to flourish in Attica consisted of farmers and mostly small-time merchants as well as the manufacturers and traders. They were independent but also interdependent individuals, disputatious and self serving but also aware of community: the ideal constituency for the institution of democracy which developed over the following hundred or so years.

The Greeks owed much to the olive. The ease with which they lived, the liberality of their public life and many of the luxuries of their private lives derived from it. And they in turn honoured the olive by giving it a divine mythology. All over Greece there were sacred olive trees – one of Solon's laws made chopping one down a capital offence – chief among them the sacred olive of Athena. The Greeks believed, or it might be more accurate to say liked to believe, that Athena and Poseidon, god of the sea, competed for the honour of presiding over Athens. Each offered a gift to the Athenians. Poseidon struck the ground with his trident and a spring gushed forth. Useful in times of siege perhaps, but the water was salt. The goddess majestically planted an olive tree and although Poseidon had been the first to reach the city Zeus forced him to share sovereignty over it with her. The tree that Athena planted does not quite still flourish, but a replica planted in the precincts of the Erectheum

The Athenian statesman Solon encouraged the city-state's farmers to grow olives. The oil they produced was highly prized all around the Mediterranean and the wealth it generated helped to create the glories of Greek civilization – drama, democracy and classical architecture. This vase, painted in c. 520 BC, shows how ripe olives were harvested by beating the branches of the tree with long sticks.

Temple on the Acropolis by the nineteenth-century equivalent of the local tourist board is an admirable stand-in.

The sacred significance of the olive stretches back beyond the Greeks and forward into the present. The fact that we call our finest grade of olive oil 'virgin' has been attributed to the oil's sacredness which required that, at some time in the dim past, only virgins could harvest the olive crop. A nice story but, as far as I can tell, one with no foundation. And if the virgins were harvesting the crop, what were the extra virgins doing?

The Old Testament is full of references to the olive beginning with the dove's return to the ark bearing an olive branch in its mouth. In the book of Judges, Jotham the youngest of the seventy sons of Jerubbaal, preached a sermon about the trees' search for a king: 'They said to the olive tree "Be king over us." But the olive tree answered: "What leave my rich oil by which gods and men are honoured, to go and hold sway over trees?"' The olive had a point because, according to Exodus, olive oil had a sacred role not lightly dismissed. Included in its catalogue of God's many instructions to Moses is the recipe for a sacred anointing oil. 'Take spices as follows: five hundred shekels of sticks of myrrh . . . two hundred and fifty shekels of fragrant cinnamon, two hundred and fifty shekels of aromatic cane, five hundred shekels of cassia by the sacred standard and a hin of olive oil.' A hin is about 12 litres (more than 2½ gallons). The recipe goes on: 'From these prepare a sacred anointing oil, a perfume compounded by the perfumer's art. This will be the sacred anointing oil.' God told Moses to anoint the Ark of the Covenant and all the liturgical lamps and vessels with the oil and to anoint Aaron and his sons with it to consecrate them as priests. The anointing oil has resonances beyond these specific injunctions to Moses in the desert. 'Christ' is derived from the Greek for 'the anointed one' and has the same root – *khriein* (to anoint) – as 'chrism' or holy oil.

Holy oil is with us still. The centrepiece of the coronation of any English monarch is the anointment, a moment which provides us with the last remnant of the concept of the divine right of kings and associates his or her role with the word of God as told to Moses. When Elizabeth II was crowned in 1953, monarchies appeared to be entering the modern age: for the first time ever television cameras were allowed to record the ceremony. But they were not permitted to film perhaps the most sacred part of the ritual when the Archbishop of Canterbury picked up the ampulla, the elaborate eagle-shaped container for the chrism, and carefully poured the oil through the eagle's beak into a gold spoon held by the Dean of Westminster. The archbishop dipped three fingers in the oil and anointed the young queen's hands and elbows, then made the sign of the cross on her forehead. The queen, the anointed one, was tangibly linked not only to Christ but also to the priests of the Old Testament.

The formula for the coronation oil remains a secret, but the Dean of Westminster revealed to the *Pharmaceutical Journal* that it, 'contains the oils of orange flowers, of roses, cinnamon, jasmin and sesame, with benzoin, musk, civet and ambergris.' It is closely related to the ancient recipe, but without an olive in sight, I regret to say. In this it is unlike the chrism still made in large quantities by the Armenian Orthodox Church to a recipe which includes nutmeg, ginger, basil, gooseberry, spearmint, rosewater, cinnamon and copious quantities of olive oil. The mixture is blessed, decanted into small bottles and sent throughout the Armenian Church world to baptise babies and consecrate priests, bishops and churches. Just as the British coronation legend bases the anointing oil on an earlier oil used to anoint the Merovingian king Clovis in the fifth century, the Armenian chrism is supposedly descended from the oil which Mary Magdalene used to bathe Christ's feet. Why oil? How can you dress a salad, anoint a king or welcome a baby into the Church with the same mixture of fatty acids, triglycerides, polyphenols and tocopherols?

Overleaf: Oil has sacred associations and the act of anointing with it as a mark of God's favour crops up throughout the Bible. In this illustration from the fifteenth-century Nuremburg Bible the prophet Samuel anoints Saul, the first king of Israel. Modern monarchs are also anointed; when Elizabeth II was crowned in 1953 this was the most secret part of an otherwise public ceremony.

Perhaps the best answer comes from the Greek priest who told me that oil, bread and wine are the ritual trinity of foods because they are products of the earth – gifts of God – that have been made with human hands.

Oil and bread are examples of what we might call sacred staples: foods whose usefulness has rendered them indispensable and transformed them from mere sustenance into part of the fabric of a particular culture. Sacred staples soon become so important that it is hard to imagine their host culture living without them or, at least, being in any way recognizable without them. What would ancient Greece have been like without oil to flavour food, bless the dead, reward the living and earn enough money to pay for at least some of the glories of classical civilization? How could the Egyptians have built the pyramids without bread to feed the labourers or to leave as offerings for the souls of dead pharaohs? When a food becomes a sacred staple it becomes wrapped in myth and ceremony: myth to lift it above its mundane origins and give it a worthy pedigree; ceremony to ensure that supernatural forces will not take it away and destroy the culture that has been built around it. But sacred staples come and go. The buffalo of the American Great Plains is probably the outstanding example of the life, death and rebirth of a sacred staple.

The extent of the Great Plains is mind-boggling: nearly a million square miles of mostly open country running in a broad belt across America from Canada to Texas; an area, nearly the size of all of Europe, which once supported the rich and varied culture of the American Plains Indians. The names are a litany of romance and adventure: the Sioux, Kiowa, Dakota, Cheyenne, Blackfoot, Pawnee and other nomadic, tribal states. And all of them were sustained by the buffalo – at one time as many as 60 million that roamed the plains. A member of the same family as domestic cattle, the buffalo (or North American bison) is hardy and well equipped to withstand the extremes of temperature in the Great Plains. Buffalo could live to twenty years and a mature specimen, weighing as much as a Rolls-Royce, was a four-legged supermarket that supplied most of the necessities of life for the Plains Indians. Tepees were made out of buffalo hides and tanned with buffalo brains, spoons and cups were fashioned out of buffalo horn, buffalo fur made warm winter robes, buffalo sinew made bowstrings and buffalo meat was delicious, low fat and full of nutrients. As the Indian writer Black Elk observes, 'The buffalo was to the Sioux the most important of all four legged animals, for it supplied their food, their clothing and even their houses . . . Because the buffalo contained all these things within himself . . . he was a natural symbol of the universe, the totality of all manifested forms.' The buffalo, Black Elk explains, symbolized the earth and the plants that grow on it, all the animals and all the peoples. Even its four legs had their symbolic values representing the Sioux idea of the four ages of mankind. Although the Plains Indians themselves slaughtered prodigious numbers of buffalo they held the animal in the highest respect and thought of it almost as a partner in life. Buffalo were often ritually slain with elaborate ceremony and many Indians believed that the dead animals would rise again ready to be hunted in the future. Their skulls were sometimes elaborately arranged awaiting their resurrection. Apart from the mid-nineteenth-century Irish and their dependency on the potato crop, almost no culture has ever relied so heavily on a single food with such tragic consequences as that of the Plains Indians of North America.

The buffalo herds of the plains were sustained by a natural pastureland of prodigious size and quality. 'Western wild grasses were unique and enjoyed a distinct advantage over the grasses of the east. They were resilient to drought and unlike the eastern grasses did not need to be "cured" in barns over winter. Western grasses dried out on the open ground, providing a rich and nourishing source of hay for winter grazing,' writes Jeremy Rifkin. Another historian called it 'wonder grass' and this wonder grass sealed the death sentence for both the great buffalo herds and the civilization of the Plains Indians.

The nineteenth-century United States was a nation with a zeal for

Overleaf: Like the oil they produce, olives are a staple food throughout the Mediterranean region. The trees that bear them flourish in thin, rocky soil and a healthy specimen will produce 20 kilograms (44 pounds) of fruit each year, sometimes for hundreds of years.

expansion; a 'manifest destiny' as the politicians called it to expand from the Atlantic Coast to the Pacific, to tame a whole continent. The California Gold Rush of 1848 had firmly established American control of the Pacific Coast. After the Union victory in the Civil War in 1865 industrial capitalism – as opposed to the slave-powered agrarianism of the South – was firmly established as the economic way forward. The swelling urban population wished to be fed on beef. The heart of the continent, home of the belligerent Plains Indians, had to be pacified to secure the overland routes to the West Coast and, by the way, wouldn't the 'wonder grass' of the Plains make the most splendid pasture for the white man's cattle? Beginning in about 1870 professional buffalo hunters, often employed by the railway companies and supported by the army, began the great extermination of the buffalo. The army commander and Civil War hero Major-General Philip Sheridan gave a blood-chilling précis of the operation. The buffalo hunters, he said, 'are destroying the Indian's commissary; and it is a well-known fact that an army losing its base of supplies is placed at a great disadvantage . . . For the sake of lasting peace let them [the buffalo hunters] kill, skin and sell until the buffalo is exterminated. Then your prairies can be covered with speckled cattle and the festive cowboy who follows the hunter as a second forerunner of an advanced civilization.' Sheridan's contrast between the cattle eaters of an advanced civilization and the savage buffalo eaters echoes Homer's disdain of 2000 years earlier when he compared olive-oil-using Greeks to 'butter-eating barbarians'.

The scale of the slaughter of the buffalo was astonishing. By 1882 an army officer could write that the Plains Indians 'are reduced to the condition of paupers, without food, shelter, clothing or any of the necessities of life which came from the buffalo'. The millions of animals had been reduced not to hundreds of thousands or tens of thousands, but to a handful. Some sources say that as few as 1000 buffalo survived the massacre. The Indians, erstwhile lords of the Plains, were confined to government reservations in conditions that ranged from the just acceptable to the squalid. Beef began to enter their diet, but 'the white man's buffalo' had a bitter taste for many.

Some historians have claimed that the buffalo population was declining as early as 1840 and we know that the Indians themselves had concerns about its future health: as Peter Matthiessen tells us, Chief Lone Horn 'had made medicine to bring about the return of the vanishing buffalo' in 1859 and buffalo were never plentiful after the early 1860s. But even if we accept hard-line interpretations of a decline in the buffalo population before the great massacre there is still no question that government policy in the years immediately after the Civil War was that the Great Plains should be made available for cattle ranching and settlement by systematically destroying the Plains Indians; and that this destruction could be accomplished most effectively by slaughtering the herds of buffalo that gave them both sustenance and identity. It was a chilling and callous example of *realpolitik* which could have fitted comfortably into the programme of any twentieth-century totalitarian state.

But the buffalo is making a comeback on the Great Plains. Herds have been steadily increasing in size since the nadir of a century ago and the current population is approaching a quarter of a million. Nostalgia for the buffalo has led to a new appreciation of the toughness of its constitution and the tenderness of its flesh. Buffalo meat is still a novelty, but it is being produced in America's western states. The day of the buffalo-burger may be upon us. More astonishing than the rise in buffalo herds was the appearance of a white buffalo calf born on a Wisconsin farm on 20 August 1994. The calf, named Miracle, was a zoological rarity – not an albino, but a dark-eyed buffalo with white fur. But Miracle's birth is of more than zoological significance. An ancient Plains Indian legend tells the story of a holy woman who appeared to the Sioux at a time of hunger and taught them how to pray and use the holy pipe. She told

Overleaf: Department stores on the hoof, American bison provided food, clothing and a rhythm to the lives of the Plains Indians. When the buffalo were destroyed by a government policy that encouraged cattle ranching, the tribes' way of life largely vanished too. But buffalo herds are returning to the western United States and buffalo-burgers are beginning to appear on some American menus.

the Sioux that she would return and was then transformed into a white buffalo calf and disappeared. The food shortage was over. The second coming of the holy woman in the form of a white female buffalo calf has been awaited for years. Perhaps Miracle's birth foretells the return to eminence of the buffalo and the Plains Indians. On some weekends as many as 4000 people visit the farm where Miracle lives. Sadly for them, little Miracle has not remained white.

As we have discussed earlier, we are what we eat and when we feel that what we eat is special or divinely ordained we invent myths and create rituals around it. But we are also what we don't eat. Dietary prohibitions are taken seriously all over the world. Eat the wrong food and you may be expelled from the group or punished by whichever god or gods you worship. The first prohibition was the apple in the Garden of Eden, symbolic of loss of innocence and the gloss of sophistication. 'You may eat from any tree in the garden,' God told Adam, 'except from the tree of the knowledge of good and evil; the day you eat from that you are surely doomed to die.' Adam behaved himself; Eve, alas, did not and the consequences were terrible. Mankind – as the couple might have been called – was driven from the Garden of Eden and told that, 'only by the sweat of thy brow will you win your bread, until you return to the earth'. All because of an apple.

The rationale behind taboo food is often fairly clear. God did not want mankind to eat the apple because it would give them a form of knowledge He did not want them to have. Fair enough. Pythagoras, the semi-mythical Greek philosopher and mathematician (who was probably not responsible for inflicting generations of schoolchildren with Pythagoras' theorem – that the square of the length of the hypotenuse equals the sum of the squares of the other two sides in a right-angled triangle), established a colony of devotees in southern Italy in the sixth century BC who devoted much time to decoding the mystical significance of music and mathematics. They were strict vegetarians. Not surprising, given their belief in the transmigration of souls. If one of your brethren is destined to return to earth as a sheep, kebabs should not be on the menu. So their belief in reincarnation created and justified their taboo against eating meat. But many food taboos resist rational explanation.

The most famous as well as the most exhaustive are the dietary instructions issued to the Israelites by God in the book of Leviticus. Many of the more specific regulations relate to offerings and sacrifices, but the foods allowed or prohibited to the followers of Moses in the course of their daily lives makes fascinating reading. The Israelites are allowed to eat any cud-chewing, cloven-hoofed animal (this includes cattle and sheep), any fish with both fins and scales and any insect with 'legs joined above their feet for leaping on the ground' (this includes locusts). Camels, rock badgers, snakes, shellfish, chameleons, thorn-tailed lizards, cormorants, owls, storks, bats and, most famously, the pig are just a few of the prohibited creatures. 'The purpose of the law,' God tells Moses, 'being to make a distinction between the unclean and the clean, between living creatures that may be eaten and those that may not be eaten.' The meaning and the strictness of the dietary laws of Leviticus have puzzled and fascinated Jew and non-Jew alike since ancient times. Why this lengthy catalogue? Why some creatures and not others? Maimonides, the medieval Jewish physician and philosopher, felt that the laws existed to 'train us in the mastery of our appetites' but added that, 'All the food which the Torah has forbidden us to eat has some bad or damaging effect on the body.' Maimonides saw a moral as well as a practical purpose to the prohibitions. Restraint was good in itself he seems to be saying and, by the way, foods we are restrained from eating are bad for us anyway. Maimonides is only one of hundreds of Jews and non-Jews who have attempted to explain the dietary laws. Functionalists believe that the laws were laid down for reasons of health and, indeed, it is tempting to see

Overleaf: The display of sausages in this shop in Barcelona shows just how culinary useful the pig is: many pork-eating societies boast that they use every part of the animal 'except the squeak'. But it is also a culturally contentious beast. Devout Jews and Muslims are forbidden to eat it and many Spanish practices related to pork butchery seem to date from the time when Muslims and Jews were expelled from Spain and eating pork became one of the badges of true 'Spanishness'.

350
300

150
160
950
850
750

the Levitican prohibitions as God's recipe for a healthy diet. But as John Cooper points out in his social history of Jewish food, *Eat and Be Satisfied*, simple functional reasons are not enough to explain the complexity of the laws. After considering Maimonides, Cooper cites another medieval rabbi who states that, 'the dietary laws are not, as some have suggested, motivated by therapeutic considerations, God forbid! Were it so, the Torah would be denigrated to the status of a minor medical treatise and worse.' Then there is the ecological interpretation of the prohibitions. Depicting God as the progenitor of Greenpeace, Mervin Harris makes a case that the forbidden animals had a harmful impact on the environment of the ancient Near East. The environmental considerations set out by Harris and others make interesting reading. Cereal production is, of course, a much more efficient way to supply a population with calories than slaughtering animals which have to graze in arid conditions or be fed cultivated grasses. And this brings us to the pig.

The pig is one of the most remarkable and valuable domesticated animals. Pork-crazy societies girdle the globe and many could boast, like the butchers of Lyon, that they use 'every part of the pig except the squeal'. But two of our oldest universal religions, Judaism and Islam, do not merely disdain the pig and its products. They actively despise them. Where does this hatred of the pig come from? Religious Jews may shun lobsters but they do not, as far as I know, hate them. The poor pig is both spurned and anathematized. Pigs, Harris says with feeling, just were not suited to life in the Middle East. They are not ruminants like cattle and find the region's tough, stalky vegetation hard to digest. They do not like the heat (contrary to the popular saying pigs *can't* sweat) and, once they are slaughtered that same heat taints their flesh rapidly. So pigs and the Middle East do not mix. Which sounds plausible except that the Egyptians raised them and remains of pigs have been found at archaeological sites throughout the region. It is, of course, easy to establish a strong group identity by not eating what everyone else around you is eating. So perhaps the shunning of the blameless pig is just another way of being different.

It is certainly a strongly felt way of being different. After Ferdinand of Aragon and Isabella of Castille had driven the ingenious and civilized Moors into exile from the Iberian Peninsula in the late fifteenth century, they turned on 'the enemy within', the Spanish Jewish community. A large number of Jews fled Spain or were expelled but a number stayed in what they considered to be their country and continued to practise their faith in secret. One way for the authorities and amateur zealots of the Catholic community to discover these hidden Jews was to create increasingly elaborate occasions for the public preparation and consumption of pig flesh. Anyone who did not enthusiastically co-operate was obviously a secretly devout Jew and a potential victim of the Inquisition. Until fairly recently – and there are still some scattered examples – slaughtering pigs and preparing hams and sausages occasioned a communal fiesta in many villages, a colourful, folkloric event which appears to have had its roots in the persecution of the Jews by Ferdinand and Isabella. What has survived is the Spanish fondness for preparing food with blood. Britain and France may have their blood sausages, but the cuisine of Spain also boasts blood pancakes. These too may be a reminder that we are what we don't eat: the Bible enjoined Jews to, 'Eat not the blood: for the blood is the life'.

Food taboos may seem quaint or sometimes downright annoying, but they are deeply felt and perilously ignored. In 1857 British forces in India were under severe pressure on a number of fronts and in order to increase their firepower the authorities issued the new and powerful Enfield rifles to the native troops serving with the British. The ammunition was supplied in paper-wrapped cartridges which had to be bitten open before the rifles could be loaded. Somehow a rumour spread that the cartridges were greased with animal fat. Muslim troops believed that abominable pig fat had been used, Hindus felt as strongly that the grease was beef fat (which was forbidden to them). The soldiers rebelled and the rebellion spread throughout the sub-continent. It took a year for the British to regain the upper hand. The British crown dissolved the East India Company which had been responsible for commercial policy and lesser administration and assumed direct control over India. In many ways 'the Great Mutiny' marked the beginning of the British Empire in India. However, it also marked the beginning of the end of that empire: the native population had realized that they could stand up and make their feelings heard.

Dining and Display

CHAPTER 3

My first great gastronomic adventure took place on a rainy Friday afternoon in early April 1959: I mixed a cocktail. I was eight years old, drinking a glass of orange juice and thought it would be more interesting if I added something to it. I rummaged through the kitchen cupboards until I was attracted by a dusty bottle distinguished by what was even then a quaint orange label. It was called Lea & Perrins Worcestershire Sauce. I carefully poured the orange juice into a bigger glass, uncapped the Lea & Perrins and decided that a 50:50 mixture of the two would be a good starting-point for my cocktail. It smelled questionable and looked awful, but so did a lot of things that adults ate and drank and raved about. I drained the glass. When I had finished throwing up, I studied the ingredients list on the orange label – a mesmerizing litany of exotic and apparently mismatched ingredients: green chillies, garlic, shallots, tamarind, cloves, molasses, anchovies . . . Anchovies? I could not help feeling that they were totally out of place. Even at the age of eight I was certain that anchovies, molasses and tamarind could not possibly be mixed into something palatable. A feeling probably shared by the Victorian high street chemists Messrs Lea, Perrins and Smith when Lord Sandys, recently retired governor of Bengal – in effect the top man in British India – asked them if they could make up an Indian recipe for relish as made by his cook back in Calcutta. Lea, Perrins and Smith concocted a few gallons and decanted it into stone storage jars. They tasted the liquid and were, to say the least, unimpressed, so put the jars aside for Lord Sandys to collect.

For some reason he never returned and two years later the jars emerged from their corner of the cellar presumably during stocktaking. The chemists tasted the revolting mixture again and found that two years' rest had transformed the Indian relish into something that was both palatable and saleable. Lea and Perrins' much copied 'Original and Genuine' Worcestershire Sauce became one of Victorian Britain's most celebrated food exports: even today 25 million litres (5½ million gallons) are manufactured every year. So, contrary to my youthful experience and Lea, Perrins and Smith's initial reservations, a concoction that included slowly decomposing – or should I say maturing – anchovies struck a universal chord. It is a historically persistent flavour and part of the universal human wish to add extra, even extraneous, flavour to food.

Every time we put ketchup on a hamburger, chutney on a cheese sandwich, soya sauce on rice or, indeed, a shot of Worcestershire Sauce ('original and genuine' or otherwise) on a shepherd's pie we are indulging a centuries-old taste. The Romans, for example, had an unbridled passion for a liquid relish they called *garum* or *liquamen.* Its strongest tasting ingredient was the innards of small fish – anchovies, as used in Worcestershire Sauce, mackerel or sprats. The fish were salted and left in the sun where they were allowed to ferment and turn into a pungent condiment. Different cooks and gourmets had their own ways of treating this basic flavouring, adding wine and various spices and seasonings. Liquamen was a big business and there were manufacturing sites all around the Mediterranean coast. Archaeologists have discovered the remains of liquamen factories in cities as far apart as Leptis Magna in Libya, Cadiz in southern Spain and Clazomenae in Asia Minor and traces of the relish have been found in *amphorae,* the elegant clay storage jars that were used throughout the Roman Empire. In spite of its extremely high price – the most expensive liquamen would have sold for the equivalent of about £1000 a litre – Romans seem to have used it in the way that Americans sometimes appear to use ketchup: on absolutely everything. Puzzlingly for our modern taste, the salty, pungent, fishy liquid even turns up in Roman recipes for puddings. Apart from Worcestershire Sauce there are numerous other descendants of liquamen, most of which are found in the Far East. The Vietnamese douse their food with *nuoc mam*, many Thai dishes call for *nam pla* and Philippine cooks reach for their bottles of *patis*. In Laos a few drops of *nuoc mam* are added to babies' bottles. Interestingly enough, the dregs of the Roman version were thought to be powerful medicine and prescribed for burns, ulcers and crocodile bites.

Although liquamen was ubiquitous in Roman cooking it was only one of many flavourings the Roman palate demanded. Cardamom, ginger, cinnamon and, above all, pepper came to Rome; and all of them had to be imported from the East. 'At the lowest reckoning,' the lawyer, statesman and natural historian Pliny the Elder complained in the first century AD, 'India, China and the Arabian peninsula take from our Empire 100 million sesterces a year.'

Along with Aristotle and Herodotus, Pliny the Elder was one of the most enquiring minds of the ancient world. He was famously so curious about the eruption of Mount Vesuvius in AD 79 that he stayed too long, and too close, to observe it and was suffocated by the volcano's sulphur fumes. Although he knew more about everything – from the working life of bees to the geography of Africa – than any man of his time, he was frankly puzzled and disturbed by the growing Roman taste for exotic flavours. 'It is amazing,' he wrote, 'that pepper is so popular. Some substances attract by their sweetness, others by their appearance, yet pepper has neither fruit nor berries to commend it. Its only attraction is its bitter flavour and to think that we travel all the way to India for it! Who was the first man willing to try this on his food, who because of his greedy appetite was not content merely to be hungry?' As far as Pliny was concerned pepper and other fanciful flavourings of Roman cookery were not just expensive and unpleasant but downright dangerous and decadent. In spite

Overleaf: This illustration from a fifteenth-century French book of wonders shows pepper being harvested in Quilon in southern India. Ever since the Romans developed a taste for the spice, the need to find and secure supplies has impelled Europeans to travel half-way around the world, laying the foundations for the growth of imperialism and the international economy.

of his success in the government of imperial Rome – he was among other things procurator or governor of Gallia Narbonensis (the South of France) and Hispania Tarraconensis (the greater part of Spain) – he viewed the ostentatious, *nouveau riche* behaviour of his fellow citizens with distaste. As the scholar John Healy observes, 'Pliny's criticism . . . of extravagant life-styles, luxury, avarice and greed is not surprising'. Provincial by birth, conservative by nature and stoic by education, Pliny felt that food was not an appropriate subject for display. His lament that honest hunger had been replaced by pretentious greed has been heard in many societies at many different times.

We shall probably never know why the Romans chose food as one of the vehicles for their most vulgar and distasteful displays of ostentation, but we do know that by doing so they set a pattern that persists in a watered-down, though no less objectionable, form today at pretentious dinner parties and restaurants. The hotel dining-room in the West Indies that advertised its steak and kidney pie as *Ragout de Boeuf Anglais en Croute* would have gladdened the heart of any Roman.

When it came to pretention and vulgarity around the dinner table the Roman emperors of the early centuries AD established a benchmark that has never been equalled. Let us pay a visit to the household of Elagabalus, the boy emperor who ruled from 218 to 221 and whose excesses were shocking even by the highest standards of imperial decadence. The imperial dining-rooms are a riot of scent and colour thanks to tens of thousands of roses, lilies, hyacinths and narcissi. The emperor and his guests are reclining. This is not decadent in itself as diners reclined throughout the ancient world, but Elagabalus was only really comfortable when his couch was made out of solid silver. Indeed, silver figured largely in the emperor's catering arrangements: all the kitchen pots and pans were solid silver and many were rather lewdly decorated. Guests are drinking huge quantities of wine flavoured with outlandish substances like pennyroyal, mastic and ground-up pine cones. When the food arrives it is almost indescribable in quantity, variety and perversity. There are familiar sights like lobsters, crabs, oysters and mussels, but they are served alongside camels' heels, cocks' combs, peacocks' tongues and wild sows' udders.

Nothing was too bizarre to delight Elagabalus. At one dinner he dished up 600 ostrich heads, at others he sprinkled fish with pearls or asked lentils to be decorated with onyx or beans with lumps of amber. There were dozens of courses and some meals lasted all day. The emperor frequently took time out for a bath in saffron-scented water or to make love to one of his many concubines of either sex. As his tastes became more and more esoteric he challenged his guests to invent dishes for him. Those who were successful were rewarded. Others, whose recipes displeased him, were condemned to eat their unsuccessful dishes until they had invented better ones. The emperor sometimes tormented his guests by serving them nothing but glass replicas of food or paintings of his favourite dishes while he himself feasted. Dining with Elagabalus was hardly a barrel of laughs. Unsurprisingly, he was murdered by his disgruntled subjects.

Many of his predecessors had also taken the pleasures of the table to baroque extremes, all of which were carefully chronicled by that arch-gossip of the Roman Empire, Gaius Suetonius Tranquillus. Suetonius tells how one first-century emperor – the sadistic and inept Vitellius – composed a dish in honour of the goddess Minerva: 'The recipe called for pike-livers, pheasant-brains, peacock-brains, flamingo tongues and lamprey-roe; and the ingredients, collected in every corner of the Empire right from the Parthian frontier to the Spanish Straits, were brought to Rome by naval captains and triremes. Vitellius paid no attention to time or decency in satisfying his remarkable appetite.' Like Elagabalus, Vitellius was murdered.

While the imperial court indulged in esoteric luxuries the average Roman continued to live as his ancestors had done on a diet that consisted mostly of

Overleaf: The Victorian painter Edward Armitage reconstructed Herod's wedding feast as a rather decorous orgy where elaborate food and drink, music and a sprinkling of sex made a statement about wealth and social status. The Romans perfected the art of conspicuous consumption as increasingly ostentatious dining and entertaining became a trademark of their upper crust.

bread, enlivened by a little fish or meat here and there, honey, oil and fruit. Between the immemorial diet of the working man and the excesses of the emperors we witness something new in ancient Rome; the development of a sophisticated cuisine as the art of cooking begins to be codified in literature. Along with civil engineering, central heating and the orgy the Romans bequeathed the cookery book to civilization.

The godfather of all cuisine, the author of the first celebrated cookery book, is the shadowy Apicius, gourmet and man of letters. We know very little about his life. He may have been one of two gourmets or even a combination of both of them. Whatever his identity, it is hardly a coincidence that Apicius began to write about cookery in the first century, in the years following the extension of Roman power into the Arabian peninsula. The destruction of the Arab monopoly on trade to the east was a culinarily happy by-product of the Emperor Augustus' vigorous military and naval campaigning. Strange spices – Pliny's hated pepper, for example – and exotic ingredients appeared with greater frequency in Roman markets and affluent gourmets, many of whom were *arrivistes* prospering from the ever-growing imperial economy, needed guidance and inspiration to use them. Along came Apicius and *De Re Coquinaria* or 'The Art of Cooking'. The cookery book has been with us ever since, a wide-ranging genre that embraces the works both of gentleman gourmets like Apicius and those of rather more everyday cooks.

Apicius' work was reprinted during the Renaissance (the first printed edition is dated 1498), but the honour of being the first printed cookery book belongs to the splendidly titled *De Honesta Voluptate et Valetudine* ('of pleasure and health') which appeared in 1475 under the authorship of Platina, a writer rather more fêted for his *Lives of the Popes* than his recipes for home cooking. What the gifted and intellectual Platina perhaps best illustrates is that for most of the last 2000 years a love and knowledge of good food has been an accepted, indeed a necessary, part of individual accomplishment. However, few people read his – or any – early cookery books these days. It often seems that concepts of good cooking and eating are so bound to a particular time and place that they fail to travel well across centuries and civilizations.

While scholars, a few restaurateurs and the merely curious have re-created many of Apicius' dishes many of the recipes appear to be wilfully perverse and over-flavoured to modern minds and tastes. A sauce for shellfish contains pepper, lovage, parsley, mint, cassia, cumin, honey, vinegar and the ever-present liquamen. A recipe for well-hung game birds calls for thyme, hazelnuts, figs, mustard, pepper, lovage, mint and more liquamen. One of Apicius' less welcome innovations was the idea of force-feeding geese to enlarge their livers. Nearly 2000 years later *foie gras* is one of the world's most bitterly reviled dishes. Many people ask themselves if it is right that animals should suffer to gratify our whimsical tastes, a question that would never have occurred to a Roman. But what drove the emperors and their courtiers to eat so preposterously? What made Apicius and the cooks he inspired so crazed for novelty that food climbed an Everest of artificiality?

Where Pliny saw honest hunger being replaced by depraved greed, we can see that food was entering the corridors of power; it was becoming an explicit element in status. The powerful are not like other people, the Romans appeared to be saying, so why should they eat like them? It is all rather reminiscent of God's injunction to Adam and Eve on the sixth day when he reminded us of our high standing in his creation by giving us 'dominion over the fish in the sea, the birds of the air and every living thing that moves on the earth'. By extension, the more preposterous, effortful and expensive the food we eat, the more it reflects our dominion, our power, our glory and our ability to command and get what we want even if it is not very tasty. Although taste is hardly absolute, I cannot believe that Elagabalus, Vitellius and their decadent contemporaries really enjoyed the food at their feasts in the way we expect to enjoy a good meal. A Roman banquet was a complicated political and social act, an exhibition of power. And as Voltaire was moved to observe, 'A depraved taste in food is gratified with what disgusts other people: it is a species of disease.' If power corrupts us, power must also corrupt our taste.

Taste is hardly absolute. My passion for gherkins makes *you* queasy; *I* will never understand how *you* can eat jelly doughnuts; *their* habit of eating raw eggs makes *us* feel sick. You can get the most vivid snapshot of relative taste by having breakfast at a big international hotel in the Far East. Britons are tucking into fried eggs and bacon, Germans pile plates high with cold ham and slices of cheese, Frenchmen bemoan that the croissants are not quite as flaky as the ones at home, Chinese carry steaming bowls of rice porridge. Thais have rice noodles with chilli and beef sauce and, of course, everyone eats the world breakfast: cornflakes.

Why we like what we like, and why we eat what we eat, are riddles with dozens of possible answers. There may be complex cultural and historical reasons or we may have physiological or psychological affinities and antipathies towards specific foods. We may on the other hand eat things just because we happen to like them. But explanations are never simple.

Take the celebrated oriental horror of dairy products. The Chinese, Japanese and some other Asians do not eat them. Cheese-making and milk-drinking play no part in their culinary world. There have been any number of functional explanations for this. The most popular is the notion that certain ethnic groups lack the enzyme which enables them to digest milk products. Equally, I have been told that historically the Chinese associate milk with the terrible famines that used to devastate China, killing millions. When food was nowhere to be found, mothers would eat grass and suckle their often quite grown-up children. So drinking milk became associated with desperation and depredation. China's neighbours and old-time enemies, the Mongols, however, are long-term nomads and hence milk-drinkers and butter-eaters. A retired British diplomat told me that until very recently travellers seeking accommodation in the wilds of Mongolia would be welcomed into a chief's

Taste is relative and reflects the culture of a particular society. Furthermore, when a whole civilization depends on the successful production of a food that food becomes the object of worship and superstition. Throughout the rice-growing countries of Asia the planting and harvesting of the grain are the subject of complex rituals. This shows an offering being made to the Balinese rice gods.

spacious *yurt* (a roundish tent) and offered a welcoming drink of fermented yak milk. Anyone who refused would immediately identify himself as coming from the dominion of the hated Chinese and presumably, in the old days, would have been given a less than warm reception. So not drinking a glass of milk was both a *faux pas* and a possible death sentence.

Food as we will see again and again is not just for eating. In the nineteenth century the American sociologist Thorsten Weblen identified what the ostentatious élite did as 'conspicuous consumption'. To paraphrase Brillat-Savarin, this means that you are not what you own, but you are what you spend. So the very rich, for example, have to declare their status with large yachts and palatial houses. The doctrine of 'if you've got it, flaunt it' is particularly suited to volatile, authoritarian societies like early imperial Rome or immature ones like the United States immediately after the Civil War because it lets everyone know, however unsubtly, your and their place in the pecking order. This 'conspicuous consumption' is something we will witness many times throughout the history of food.

The phenomenon flourishes all around the world today from the South of France to Beverly Hills by way of many less obvious places. Nowhere is it more extreme or more surprising than in Japan, whose modern economic success seems to be built on virtues we might characterize as puritanical: hard work, conformity and modesty. Scarcely ones we associate with vulgar display or bizarre ostentation, but some of the food rituals of modern Japan are as captivating as the banquets of imperial Rome.

'I'd rather die than eat that,' is a common enough expression, thankfully rarely taken too literally. In Japan, one of the most highly prized foods – *fugu* – is esteemed precisely because it can kill you. Eat an improperly prepared dish of fugu, whether served raw as sashimi or stewed with vegetables and tofu, and your fingers and toes will start to feel cold, your mouth will tingle, you will be racked with cramps and your breathing will become shallow and laboured. Most fugu restaurants keep the number of an emergency doctor by the telephone. But why bother calling? The poison works too quickly.

Fugu is a fish: a member of the *Tetraodontidae* family, also known as a globefish or puffer, it is found in warm waters all round East Asia. Its outstanding characteristic is its ability to quickly increase its size when threatened by a predator by pumping water into its highly elastic abdominal sacs. If this mighty morphin power-ranger trick fails to deter the attacker the puffer can secrete a poison known as tetraodontoxin which is considerably more powerful than cyanide. It is synthesized in the puffer's liver and ovaries and, like many fish toxins, attacks the central nervous system causing paralysis and death in about 50 per cent of all cases. Each fugu packs enough tetraodontoxin to kill thirteen adult humans. Rather more than most sea creatures, the attractive and rather shy puffer is magnificently well equipped to deter and destroy its predators. Eating it is a Japanese culinary obsession. A culinary obsession that sometimes ends in death.

In 1975 Mitsugoro Bando had reached the absolute peak of his profession, designated by the Japanese government as a 'Living National Treasure'. He was widely celebrated as one of the century's greatest practitioners of the art of kabuki, the highly stylized Japanese classical drama. After a performance he and three friends ordered fugu liver at a Kyoto restaurant. When the dish was set on the table Mitsugoro's companions lost their nerve and he ate all four portions. Shortly afterwards he collapsed and died. The chef at the restaurant was given an eight-year suspended sentence. (He got off lightly. Fugu chefs who kill their customers are traditionally expected to commit suicide.) Bando's was the most famous recent fugu death but as many as ten Japanese die every year from fugu poisoning, almost all of them from eating fish prepared at home. Restaurants that serve fugu are strictly regulated. Chefs who prepare it undergo an intensive training course of at least six months and many fail the

Overleaf: *Fugu* or pufferfish is a Japanese delicacy that contains enough poison to kill thirteen people. Skilled chefs train for years in order to prepare it safely but every year some gourmets flirt unsuccessfully with death on a plate. Almost all fatalities from eating the fish are the result of amateur home cooking.

examination when they take it for the first time. However, a Nagasaki businessman died in a fugu restaurant in 1992 and the mystique of sudden death is critical to the attraction of eating the fish. Reports of its flavour vary from bland to extremely delicate and texturally superb, but most fugu literature is about the thrill of dicing with death. One poem says, 'Yesterday I ate fugu, but today I am still alive' and a proverb warns us that, 'Fugu is very delicious, but I also want to live'. Regional nicknames for the fish are also full of gallows – or perhaps we should say restaurant – humour. In Kyushu, for example, they are called *gamba* which means coffin.

In reality the risk of death from poisoning in a licensed restaurant is statistically insignificant, but the fugu's extremely high price – a fugu lunch costs around £150 because the fish have to be caught on a line as net fishermen are afraid to handle them – and baneful reputation make eating it a thrilling and status-enhancing experience.

Why do the Japanese eat fugu? Perhaps because they can. As the ethnologist Jane Cobbi points out, the proper preparation of the fish requires surgical subtlety on the part of the chef and an extremely high degree of knife-making technology. So fugu involves a degree of technical showing off that fits perfectly with the Japanese love of skilful craftsmanship.

Although some restaurants breed fugu in tanks throughout the year, winter is the season for eating them. It is also the time when many non-fugu-eating Japanese face another form of culinarily induced death, this time from *O mochi*, the sticky pounded rice dish that traditionally sees in the New Year. A number of celebratory dishes, from soup to pudding, feature it. It's traditionally made by pounding rice with a hammer but, increasingly, Japanese families own electric O mochi mixers or buy 'instant' or boil-in-the-bag versions. O mochi is associated with the full moon. When Japanese children look up into the night sky they do not see a man in the moon as Westerners do; they see a rabbit making rice cake. The stickiness that distinguishes O mochi from other forms of rice is what makes it a dangerous food. In spite of television warnings about taking care when eating it, news reports of people – usually elderly – choking to death as a result of incautious O mochi eating are a regular feature of New

Year celebrations in Japan. However, New Year without a special form of rice would be unthinkable. After all, it is associated with luck and prosperity throughout East Asia. Understandably so.

The way of life of over a billion people depends on rice. The shape of their societies, and perhaps even the tenets of their religious and philosophical beliefs, have been formed by the demands of its cultivation. Rice is willing to grow from Indonesia to Japan and from sea-level to 3000 metres (10 000 feet). But it requires care and huge amounts of labour. It is the ideal crop for sustaining, some might even say encouraging, the dense populations of Asia.

The status of rice in Asia is even higher than that of bread in Western societies and is reflected proverbially in dozens of ways. In China, for example, if you lose your job you have 'broken your rice bowl'. Business deals and happy marriages are sealed over cups of sake or rice wine in Japan – its very name has a serendipitous link with the word *sakae* or prosperity. In Thailand, members of the royal family participate in a highly formalized planting and harvesting of each year's rice crop. Indeed, Thai popular mythology looks back to an Edenic era of earthly perfection in which man could live on rice alone without the need to debase it by adding condiments or other flavourings. The need to cultivate and, consequently, to respect rice has been so strong for so long that even countries that do not grow it have adopted some of the beliefs that flourish around the crop. In the West we throw confetti, symbolizing rice, for good luck at weddings. So you can see why the Japanese, in spite of all the health warnings, are loath to drop their favourite form of rice from their New Year celebrations.

Whether or not the flavour of fugu or the chewiness of O mochi is worth the chance, however slim, of death is perhaps something that only the Japanese can understand. On the other hand, a Japanese observing British eating habits might well be puzzled that, in a country with a high rate of heart disease, people enthusiastically tuck into food laced with saturated fat. In reality a pork pie or a ploughman's lunch might be more dangerous than a helping of the 'deadly' fugu fish.

Salt of the Earth

The greatest of many great landmarks in my home town of Boston is the State House or capitol building: a great Palladian palace of government built by the gentleman architect Charles Bulfinch and opened for business in 1798. I spent a lot of time there as a small boy, thanks to my favourite uncle's long and colourful career in the government of the Commonwealth of Massachusetts. It was and is a marvellous building, full of contradictions and surprises. It is typically American – the United States Capitol, also designed by Bulfinch, and most state capitols copy it in one form or another – yet it is based on the design of Somerset House in London. It is in America's most puritanical and restrained city, but its great dome is covered with 16 kilograms (35 pounds) of gold leaf.

The House of Representatives where my uncle sat for the early part of his career is a magnificent, mahogany panelled chamber, a great ellipse four storeys high. The frieze above the room is inscribed with the names of fifty-three great men of Massachusetts. It is quite a list and includes Benjamin Franklin (printer, patriot and polymathic inventor of bifocal glasses and the lightning rod), Henry Wadsworth Longfellow (poet), Samuel F. B. Morse (inventor of the telegraph), William Lloyd Garrison (apostle of the anti-slavery movement), Nathaniel Hawthorne (novelist) and John Singleton Copley (painter and member of the Royal Academy). Yet exalted above them all is a fish. A fish known without a trace of irony as the Sacred Cod.

Nearly 1½ metres (5 feet) long and carved from a block of solid pine, the

Sacred Cod has been displayed in the Massachusetts House of Representatives since the mid-eighteenth century. When the House moved from one room in the State House to another in 1895, 'the Sergeant at Arms and a committee of fifteen men, lowered the emblem, wrapped it in an American flag, placed it on a bier borne by four messengers, and escorted it to the new House chamber where it was deposited on a table in front of the Speaker's desk'. There was great applause from the assembled legislators and grandees as the fish was installed in its new home. Cod was the first export from the fledgling colony of Massachusetts to the Old World and the Atlantic cod fishery laid the foundation of the state's wealth and influence. After a morning spent with my uncle in the State House we would walk down to a restaurant called Dini's Sea Grill on Tremont Street and lunch seriously in the company of other legislators and government officials. Our lunch would be schrod, a totem dish of Boston: small cod grilled with butter and breadcrumbs.

It is hard to overstate the significance of cod in the shift of history from the Old World to the New. Just off the north-east coast of North America, and close to both New England and the maritime provinces of Canada, is a broad, submerged and rather shallow plateau that rises up from the colossal (in some places as great as 5000 metres/16 500 feet) depths of the North Atlantic. It is known as the Grand Banks and is a gathering ground for millions and millions of fish: until the discovery and exploitation of the oil fields of the Middle East, these fisheries were probably the greatest single natural resource in the history of the world. What Kuwait, Saudi Arabia, Iraq, Iran and the Arab Emirates are to petroleum the Grand Banks and their tons of codfish are to food.

The cod is a highly useful fish. Now elevated in gastronomy because of rising prices and sadly dwindling stocks it was for centuries the closest mankind has ever had to a staple, commodity fish. Prolific breeders (one female produces about 5 million eggs) and unfussy eaters (cod will feed on more or less whatever is swimming around them) their powerful bodies contain a high proportion of delicious, easily filleted white flesh. But until the development of canning, refrigeration and freezing (all of which happen much later in our story) it was notoriously difficult to keep cod – or any fish – fresh. If you have ever compared the taste of a freshly caught mackerel with one cooked later in the day or, even worse, one that has been in a shop for a couple of days, you will know that it deteriorates very, very rapidly. Of course, not all fish goes off as quickly as mackerel, but even the most resilient of them forcefully illustrate the proverbial remark that 'fish and guests stink after three days'.

Sometime in the Middle Ages the Scandinavians who fished for cod on their side of the North Atlantic found a way of preserving it by drying. The resulting product, known as stockfish, found favour all over Europe particularly in the hot countries around the Mediterranean: you can still find *stoccafisso* on many Italian menus. Unlike fresh fish, it has to be carefully soaked before being cooked or eating it will be like digging into a slab of chipboard.

Why was this fish so popular throughout medieval Europe? Largely, I suppose, because of the restrictions on meat-eating imposed by the Church. The forty days of Lent and every Friday of the year were meatless and stockfish was the answer for those not living on the coast. But while dried fish was good, fish that had been salted and then dried was even better. And cod was also ideal for this method.

The first recorded European voyages of discovery to North America – and the fisheries off its coast – were made under the leadership of the 'English' navigator John Cabot (real name: Giovanni Caboto). It is possible that Bristol merchants trading with Iceland may have been blown off course to what became known as the New World as early as the 1480s, but Cabot's landfall at Cape Breton Island in June 1497 was the first official European sighting of

Overleaf: Since the eighteenth century a carved wooden codfish has presided over the legislative business of the state of Massachusetts. Known with scant irony as the Sacred Cod, it commemorates the role cod played in the early development of New England. Every year thousands of tons were caught, salted and shipped to Europe to provide a source of protein that could survive the warm weather of Mediterranean countries. Salt cod also fed slaves in South America.

KNOX • LINCOLN • JOHN ADAMS • DANE • QUINCY • J Q ADAMS

CHOATE • PARSONS • SHAW • STORY

North America. Cabot never returned from a second voyage in 1498, but one of his children, Sebastian, carried on exploring the north-west Atlantic, as did the Portuguese brothers Gaspar and Miguel Corte Real in their voyages of 1500, 1501 and 1502. Like John Cabot, Gaspar was lost at sea. All these early explorers were impressed by the abundance of fish they found off the newly discovered coastline and a third Corte Real brother, Gaspar Annes, was canny enough to begin exploiting these new fisheries while remaining safely at home in Lisbon. So by the early years of the sixteenth century, long before any European settlement of North America, fishermen from Spain, Portugal, France and Britain were making the frightening but profitable voyage across the Atlantic and returning with holds bulging with cod. Fish later became a powerful economic tie between Europe and North America and the desire to secure those valuable Grand Banks fishing rights became, and has remained to this day, a matter of considerable political contention.

The fishing industry grew steadily thanks to Europe's expanding population and growing hunger for easily stored, long-lasting salt cod from North America. Estimates of catches are notoriously unreliable but give a strong impression of how the cod fishery boomed. In 1550 about 40 000 tons of the fish were landed. This figure had doubled to 80 000 tons by 1650 and by 1700 it had reached 100 000 tons a year. We have already seen how the Romans shipped grain across their empire and created the first international market for a foodstuff. The development of the cod fishery went one step further as salt cod – a staple of the European diet – was increasingly processed a quarter of the world away from the consumers who would make a meal of it. If interdependency and internationalism are two of the most outstanding features of today's world, cod was the commodity that first helped the world to shrink.

It became the great impetus to exploit the waters of the north-west Atlantic and then to settle the adjacent coast. These first permanent European settlements in North America were tentative and dangerous affairs. The small group of English Protestant dissenters known as the Pilgrims settled at Plymouth on the coast of Massachusetts in 1620. There were just over one hundred, and half of them died during the miserable winter of 1620–21. The turning point for this colony on the brink of extinction came in March 1621 when the survivors were terrified by the sight of an Indian warrior – a member of the Abenaki tribe – who appeared in the midst of their village. As the Pilgrims reached for their weapons the Indian, whose name was Samoset, disarmed them by announcing, 'Welcome Englishmen'. He had learnt some English from visiting cod fishermen and returned to the Pilgrim colony shortly afterwards with his friend Tisquantum, commonly known as Squanto. Squanto spoke English beautifully. He had been kidnapped years before, sold into slavery in Spain and then escaped to England where he lived in the household of a well-off merchant and polished his language before returning to Massachusetts by way of Newfoundland. Squanto became the mediator between the Pilgrims and the local Indian tribes and taught the colonists enough native fishing and agricultural lore to enable them to establish themselves. His help was commemorated in the autumn of 1621 when the settlers invited the Indians to a three-day feast – a lavish ritual meal that combined Indian traditions of giving thanks with the English harvest festival. Cod was certainly on the menu. But what about turkey, the culinary icon of all subsequent Thanksgiving dinners? It was on the menu too, but hardly in a starring role: pork and fish were just as popular.

Cod generated much of the money that enabled the fledgling colonies of the New World to flourish and expand. And what enabled it to become an international commodity was a simple substance we hardly even bother to think about: salt.

We literally cannot live without salt. We need between 6 and 10 grams a day (¼ to ⅓ ounce), depending on the temperature, if our bodies are to function

Overleaf: The great fisheries off the eastern coasts of North America were – and still are – one of the greatest natural resources ever exploited by man. The lure of these rich seas stimulated the exploration of the Americas, and the wealth fish brought to the British colonies was a powerful factor in creating the basis of the American economy.

properly. We would also find it hard to enjoy food without it. Even more so than sugar, it is mankind's favourite flavouring. It is not a spice, nor is it really a food. It is a combination of two elements, sodium and chlorine that we humans both want and need to consume. There are just over a hundred elements, the building blocks of our world, and sodium is the sixth most common one. When it combines with chlorine, which is less common but hardly exotic, the result is sodium chloride – chemical symbol NaCl – known to us as common salt. Basically two types of common salt have sustained human demands: sea salt and rock salt. Sea salt is formed by the evaporation of sea water: one cubic mile (1313 cubic metres) contains enough salt to satisfy the entire population of the world for a year. Rock salt lies in large deposits underground, the dried remnants of ancient seas. Salt can also be made by evaporating the water from briny springs.

While the production of salt by evaporation is fairly straightforward, mining it was a dangerous and heroic enterprise. At Wieliczka, just outside the university town of Crakow in southern Poland, salt has been mined since the late thirteenth century. When Casimir the Great of Poland founded Crakow University in 1364 he ordered that its professors be paid with income produced by the mines. These are almost an underground city. Two visitors writing in 1912 observed in amazement that, 'The whole place is one huge block of salt. The galleries carved out of salt are sometimes twice as high as the vault of a church. These vast galleries lead to great squares, chapels, houses, sheds and stables made of salt.' Even the altar candlesticks in the chapel of the Blessed Kinga are carved out of salt: marriages carried out there are said to be particularly enduring, a testimony to salt's frequent role as a symbol of friendship. There is also a sanatorium 211 metres (700 feet) underground where patients breathe the salty air that is reputed to be good for asthma and bronchitis.

Wherever they exist salt mines are prodigies of size and engineering. Just over a thousand years ago in Han dynasty China, they reached depths of 150 metres (500 feet). Salt brine was transported through bamboo pipelines that could be up to 11 kilometres (7 miles) long.

In 1968 BBC Radio carried an item about a temporary sugar shortage in British shops. Disc jockey Jimmy Young asked one of his guests what the next shortage would be and the joking reply was 'salt'. Panic-stricken shoppers went into a frenzy of salt-buying the next day and cleared shop shelves. They were not aware that Cheshire mines alone contain 4000 million tons of salt. However, salt is not distributed evenly around the world and getting it from the places that have it to the people who want it has built fortunes and even empires.

Fifth-century Italy was a terrifying and confusing place in which to live as the Roman Empire spiralled into terminal decline, racked from within by uncontrollable social and economic problems and battered from without by energetic and rapacious barbarian – that is, not Roman – enemies. Attila the Hun hit Italy with the subtlety of a horse falling off a cliff in 452. Among the casualties of his conquest was Aquileia. The greatest city of the northern Adriatic, and once the ninth greatest in the Roman Empire, it had been sacked 50 years earlier by Alaric and his Goths. Its Christian residents fled from their conquerors and found refuge in the small islands scattered through the shallow, brackish lagoons of the north-eastern Italian coast. The new settlers continued their immemorial occupations of fishing off the Adriatic coastline and making salt from evaporated sea water. A contemporary writer, Cassiodorus, wrote: 'All your energies are spent on your salt fields; in them indeed lies your prosperity and your power to purchase those things which you have not. It may be that some seek not gold, but there lives not a man that does not need salt.'

No matter who ruled Italy, Roman or barbarian, salt was needed on the table and the islanders prospered in their new homes. They had to develop the

Overleaf: These Vietnamese workers are gathering salt that has been produced by evaporation. Although their task is back-breaking, it is not dangerous – unlike that of labourers who mine salt formed underground. In Han dynasty China salt mines were as much as 150 metres (500 feet) deep.

skills to market the salt they produced as well as fleets to ship it in and protect it. Within a few generations of fleeing the Goths and the Huns, the residents of the little settlements were becoming rich and formidable. They were also learning to act together politically. As the historian Edward Gibbon wrote some 1300 years later, 'In the midst of the waters, free, indigent, laborious and inaccessible they gradually coalesced into a republic.' The rise of Venice had begun. The lessons learned from the salt trade in the dark days of collapsing Rome were to be applied to the spice trade with the East. The fabulous amount of money that was made created La Serenissima, the serene republic, the most beautiful city in the world. And it all began with salt.

As Venetian expertise in the sale and distribution of salt grew, Venice began to seek control over other sources of supply. The Serene Republic was determined to monopolize the Adriatic salt trade and major Italian producers like the town of Chioggia (after Venice the second most important port of the northern Adriatic and now celebrated for its mussels) were brought into the Venetian salt network by force or diplomacy. Queen of the Adriatic, Venice occupied an incredibly advantageous position in terms of trade. Trade routes from all of central Europe descended to her by way of the Alps, and the Adriatic, transformed into a Venetian lake, was the opening to the wider world of the Mediterranean and the East. As the salt trade grew money poured into the *Camera del Sale*, the government department which collected the revenues it produced. The Camera became one of the republic's main banks and paid for wars and public works.

The sophisticated, lucrative trade in salt was not a Venetian, or even a European, prerogative. In Ethiopia, high heat and low humidity is a formula for the easy production of salt and it became an important part of the country's economy during the first to eighth centuries – the Aksumite period. It was formed into half kilogram (one pound) bars and used as currency as well as a trade commodity, transported by great caravans of camels, mules or donkeys – long trains of as many as 700 beasts, all loaded with salt, were not uncommon. Because of the value of the load they carried the caravans were organized with military precision and were heavily protected. The network of routes criss-crossed Africa. From Timbuktu, salt made the arduous journey across the Sahara to Morocco and Europe. It is no longer a currency, but salt bars are still bartered for other goods in Ethiopia.

Salt and money have long been intimately linked. People who go to work are paid a salary because a Roman soldier was given a *salarium* – a sum of money with which to buy salt. If you are a person of value to your employer you are worth your salt. This does not sound impressive in contemporary terms when salt is among our cheapest purchases, but it is deeply flattering when you consider that it has at times been dizzyingly expensive – sometimes even worth its weight in gold. It is hardly surprising, therefore, that salt has been one of the most consistently taxed commodities throughout history; and that taxes on a commodity both so desirable and so necessary should have aroused fierce opposition. Among the most hated of the monarchy's impositions in pre-Revolutionary France was the *gabelle* or salt tax. The mass of the population, already condemned by poverty to a monotonous and unexciting diet, were often driven to revolt by attempts to charge yet more for the one commodity that made their food tolerable. The hated tax was the result of the political ambitions of Charles, Count of Anjou, in the thirteenth century. He keenly wanted to add the kingdom of Naples to his already impressive list of territories, but did not have the necessary funds. Fortunately his wife's dowry included Provence, one of the great suppliers of salt, and Charles announced that henceforth all the salt produced there was to be sold to him at a price set by him. Then, like any modern speculator, he sold it at the highest price the market could bear, made his money and went on to seize Naples. Philippe of

Overleaf: The routes of the caravans that carried salt criss-crossed Africa. Everyone wanted it but only a few countries could produce it and the journey from source to customer was arduous. The tablets of salt that were slung across the backs of the camels were so valuable that until very recently they were used as money in some regions. This illustration shows a modern caravan crossing a West African desert.

France was inspired by Charles' success and the salt tax entered French history. It was brutally enforced and consumers were often obliged to buy a certain amount of salt each year. Salt was sometimes sold for as much as twenty times its cost because of the tax and the bloody rebellions and bloody repression the *gabelle* inspired punctuate French history. Toussaint-Samat tells us that in 1780 alone, 'there were 3700 seizures of contraband salt and 2300 men were arrested on the roads. So were 1800 women and 6000 children . . . 2000 people were given prison sentences and 300 were sent to the galleys for life.' That is for one year alone. The Revolutionary Government abolished the salt tax, but Napoleon reintroduced a small one and until 1945 the French paid two centimes tax for every kilo (two pounds) of salt they bought.

The excesses of the *gabelle* as administered by the *ancien régime* seem so cruel and arbitrary that they belong to another world, but we only have to look back less than seventy years to find another example of the state control of salt causing revolution. In 1930 the manufacture or selling of salt throughout India required a licence from the British authorities. Mahatma Gandhi, the most well-known of the activists agitating for Indian independence, was already famous for his development of *satyagraha* or civil resistance as a weapon in the struggle for political change. He convinced his colleagues that a major campaign of civil resistance should be launched to confront the imperial government and decided that the issue should be the salt tax. Why salt? In the words of Gandhi's biographer, Judith Brown, it was an 'ingenious resolution of many of the problems of staging a non-violent confrontation with the government on high moral ground. It did not touch Indian vested interests (which inhibited so many possible strategies), nor was salt revenue vital to the government, so harsh reprisals were unlikely. It was a highly emotive issue – a tax by an alien regime on a basic necessity of life, on which there was a long tradition of Indian political opposition to the Raj.' Brown points out that salt was also an issue of equal importance to Muslim and Hindu alike.

In March 1930 Gandhi and a small group of followers set off from the ashram at Ahmedabad and began a month-long 385 kilometre (240 mile) walk to the coast at Dandhi near Bombay. In towns and villages along the way Gandhi lectured thousands about the principles of home rule and civil disobedience. On 6 April 1930 he and his fellow protesters were on the beach at Dandhi. Gandhi picked up a muddy lump of salt from the beach, symbolically breaking the law. His followers did the same. In a photograph they are smiling and in high spirits. Later, they began boiling sea water and making their own salt. A month later Gandhi was arrested and imprisoned. But the power and authority of the Raj had been brought into disrepute and ridicule. The empire had begun to crumble. Just as salt raised Venice to its eminence, so it helped to break up the British Empire. Salt is not just money but power too. What gave it that power?

To answer that question we have to understand the conditions in which most people lived in most places in most times. A historian hardly has to be a radical to observe, as J. H. Plumb did, that the material life has never been easy for the great mass of people. It is hard for those of us who live in privileged, affluent societies to realize that even today subsistence is the rule for many, and privation a constant fear. Mankind's greatest concern has perhaps been not so much what is eaten but that there is anything at all to eat. Survival rather than gastronomy has been, and sadly remains, the rule for most. As the French historian Fernand Braudel observes, 'Refinement, variety or even having enough to eat were for the rich.' Writing of French peasants in the fifteenth and sixteenth centuries he says: 'The peasant often sold more than his "surpluses" and above all, he never ate his best produce: he ate millet and maize and sold his wheat; he ate salt pork once a week and took his poultry, eggs, kids, calves and lambs to market. As in China, feasting on special occasions interrupted the monotony and shortages of everyday life.' Monotony is on the menu almost everywhere one looks.

Much of our material on the diet of the average man and woman comes from France because historians like Braudel and his followers have been especially concerned with the history of everyday life. Emmanuel Le Roy Ladurie's scholarship on the life of peasants in the Languedoc is illuminating. This sunny, beautiful region is now a prime holiday playground, a dreamy land for tourists, studded with famous destinations like Nimes, Carcassone and

Montpellier. Its medieval workers, however, lived largely on barley, sometimes eaten as porridge, sometimes made into bread 'heavy and hard to digest even after repeated sifting'. It was not, I must stress, a time when you could say, 'Oh no, not barley bread again. I think I'll have X instead.' Because there was no X, no alternative. Imagine a life built around barley bread and barley porridge, barley porridge and barley bread, day in, day out, without the glimmer of a change. The Languedoc diet was luxurious, though, compared to that of people who lived in the hills of the Cévennes. 'The chestnut of the Cévennes was an all purpose fruit in the sixteenth century,' Le Roy Ladurie tells us. It was eaten 'raw or well pared, dried and cooked or else pounded into flour and made into bread that was black as coal . . . The Cévennes of the sixteenth century were still, and were long to remain, an ill-nourished "land without bread", a member of that wretched international community of chestnut eaters stretching from the highlands of the Estremadura to the mountains of the Rouergue and Savoy.' If a sixteenth-century diet seems remote consider that of the residents of the Swiss canton of Bern in the mid-nineteenth century when western Europe was on the verge of being recognizably modern. Bern is rich in statistics and as Christian Pfister, who teaches at the university there, points out the canton's agricultural production in 1847 would have met the standards agreed by the United Nation's Food and Agricultural Organization and the World Health Organization in 1973. So what was on the menu? Pfister tells us: 'In poor households, potatoes and turnips were the staple food: bread was liked as a dessert. Coffee was a common drink. Often milk had to be bought from farmers in the neighbourhood. The diet of the poor seems to have been

The right to produce and sell salt has often been heavily taxed and jealously guarded by governments. When Mahatma Gandhi wished to find a cause that would unite all Indians against British rule he turned to the Raj's control of this essential element. In *Gandhi* Richard Attenborough recreated the scene where the Indian leader and his followers dramatically defied the government salt monopoly on 6 April 1930.

low in fat: butter was a scarce resource, lard an object of aspiration, a symbol of something unattainable.' He records that even on prosperous farms, 'special dishes such as roasted meat or eggs were a privilege of the farmer and his wife.' It is a boring bill of fare. But almost wherever we look the daily bread of most people is hypnotically dull, and while there are treats there are also times of great privation, hunger and fear. Salt is like a gastronomic bombshell in this world of root vegetables or barley or porridge or bread – of diets that are unchanging from cradle to a sometimes early grave. It makes the inevitable palatable if not necessarily delicious.

While the casual and indeed even extravagant use of salt was the prerogative of the rich – the beautiful and elaborate gold or silver medieval and Renaissance salt cellars remain as tangible evidence – it was also an important part of the diet of the poor. Its preservative powers were widely used to add variety and vitamins to the even more drab than usual winter diet. The Middle European fondness for sauerkraut is a hangover from the days when salting and fermenting were the only ways to ensure a supply of vegetables during the winter months when the ground was often covered in snow. Salted fermented cabbage has been a mainstay of Middle European peasant diets since the technique of salting and fermenting was discovered in ancient Gaul. The same technique was applied to fodder and provided winter silage for farm animals. Today it is ironic to see this subsistence dish, combined with expensive ingredients like turbot, on the menu of up-market Parisian restaurants.

On the other side of the world, in Korea, a close relative of sauerkraut called *kim chi* has long seen Korean families through difficult winters and is now served in various rarefied forms as an almost indispensable accompaniment to even the grandest dinners. Like sauerkraut, kim chi takes cabbage, salts it, adds a number of flavours ranging from ginger to chilli to dried shrimps and lets the fermentation of lactic acid do its work. A former British ambassador to Korea told me that the annual making of kim chi was an important event in the life of every Korean family. The prepared kim chi is put into large Ali-Baba-type jars which are buried underground and unearthed as required. At the British embassy they were stored under the tennis court!

Without salt and salted food how could the monotony of so many diets have been endured? Small wonder that the lack of salt or its high cost could move people to riot or rebellion.

Salt's universal appeal means that it inevitably acquired a divine ancestry and spiritual attributes. In ancient Cyprus, Aphrodite was born out of the sea foam and washed ashore at Paphos where she was worshipped as the goddess of both love and salt in festivities that put salt-eating on the orgiastic menu. Plutarch believed it made animals eager for copulation, 'and perhaps for that same reason they call a surprising and bewitching beauty, such as apt to entice, "saltish"'. Salt played a rather different role in Christianity. Until 1974, when the reform of the liturgy pointed out that new-born babies were not to be regarded as being possessed by the devil, Roman Catholic baptisms used salt as, in the words of the sacrament, 'a salutary and effective means of putting Satan to flight. Wherefore O Lord our God, we beseech thee to sanctify this salt and bless it, and make of it a sovereign remedy to linger within the innermost being of all who partake of it.' In the gospel according to Saint Matthew, Christ called his followers 'the salt of the earth' and in Leonardo da Vinci's *The Last Supper* Judas gives the game away by knocking a salt cellar over with his elbow.

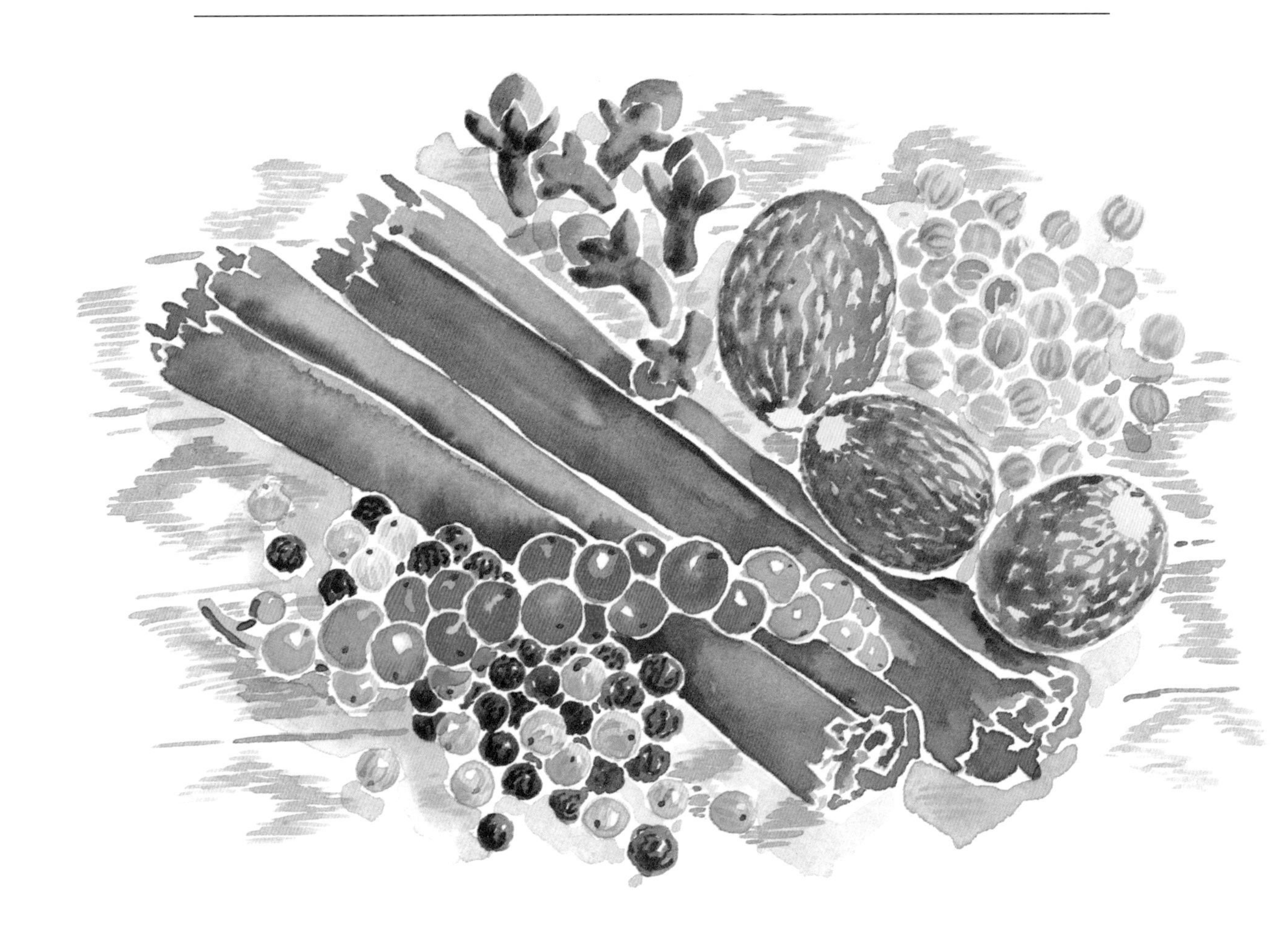

Spices of Life

CHAPTER 5

Violet Oon, a very good cook in Singapore, was showing me how to make a dish of stir-fried beef with chilli and garlic. She put a few drops of oil into a very hot wok, swirled it around and then threw the chillies in. 'How long do you cook the chillies for?' I asked. She answered that you should fry them until the cook starts crying. Within a few minutes we were both in tears as the volatile oils from the chillies were released by the intense heat. Violet wiped her eyes and carried on cooking.

There are hundreds of different sorts of chillies: green and red, big and small, relatively mild and dangerously hot. They can make you cry not only when you cook them, but also when you eat them. Some are so potent that it is wise to wear rubber gloves when preparing them – they can irritate the skin so much that you feel a true burning sensation. You either have the taste for chillies or not. I do. Although they are associated particularly with the cooking of South-east Asia and India they came from the Americas and, like many other New World products, were quickly integrated into cooking around the world. But that is a different story that we shall come to later.

There is a wonderful scene in *Vanity Fair* when Thackeray's manipulative heroine, Becky Sharp, is invited to lunch by the Sedley family. Among the guests is Joseph Sedley on leave from his job with the East India Company. As he tucks into a curry Becky asks to try some: '"Do you find it as good as everything else from India?" said Mr Sedley. "Oh, excellent!" said Rebecca, who was suffering tortures with the cayenne pepper. "Try a chilli with it, Miss

Sharp," said Joseph, really interested. "A chilli," said Rebecca, gasping. "Oh yes!" She thought a chilli was something cool, as its name imported, and was served with some. "How fresh and green they look!" she said and put one into her mouth. It was hotter than the curry; flesh and blood could bear it no longer. She laid down her fork. "Water, for Heaven's sake, water," she cried. Mr Sedley burst out laughing . . .' It is one of the very few times one feels sorry for the really quite awful Becky. That, by the way, was in the 1840s long before the proliferation of curry restaurants and Indian take-aways accustomed British palates to hotter flavours. Chilli – the fruit of pungent varieties of the *Capsicum* family – is probably the most violent of all the spices in the world's store cupboard.

I very much doubt that there is any medical evidence to say so, but spices are addictive. Unlike salt, which we need in order to stay alive, we can live without them. But once we are used to them we cannot do without them. Our collective historical addiction to cinnamon, nutmeg, black pepper and other spices has powerfully influenced human behaviour.

A Eurocentric description of these addictive substances is that they are edible, aromatic plant products that do not grow in Europe or indeed in any temperate zone. So they are by definition exotic. They are also botanically and agriculturally diverse and fascinating. Spices may be cultivated as garden crops which require regular tending or as permanent crops whose plants will produce for years and years with relatively little attention. Some spices are seeds (mustard), others are fruits (pepper) or buds (cloves). Cinnamon, which is hardly indispensable to us but pleasant enough in cookies, cakes and pies is an example of a spice that is the bark of a tree – an evergreen that can grow to 10 metres (33 feet) but which is usually coppiced to keep it to a more easily managed 2–3 metres (6½–10 feet). It is native to Sri Lanka but has spread to Seychelles and Madagascar. Cinnamon is one of the spices used in the Old Testament to make the holy anointing oil described in Chapter Two and is also romantically described in Proverbs: 'I have perfumed my bed with myrrh, aloes, and cinnamon. Come let us take our fill of love until the morning: let us solace ourselves with loves.' When Nero murdered his wife Poppea he burnt

Rome's entire stock of the spice on her funeral pyre as a token of imperial remorse. Cinnamon, holy and poetical – and we use it for cookies, cakes and pies. Could this be a crisis of *our* imagination?

Most people have little glass bottles of spices, bought relatively cheaply in supermarkets and stored in decoratively twee spice racks. Seeing them so thoroughly domesticated makes it hard to imagine that until comparatively recently they were staggeringly expensive and that obtaining them was a matter of life and death and grave political deliberation.

Like Joseph Sedley in *Vanity Fair* and thousands of other young Englishmen in the nineteenth century, Thomas Stamford Raffles went to Asia to make his fortune and add to the lustre of Britain's expanding global power. He went first to India, was posted to Java from there and was then appointed lieutenant-governor of the obscure and humid colony of Bengkulu on the south-west coast of the island of Sumatra. It was, Raffles said in a letter to a friend, 'without exception the most wretched place I ever beheld.' But Bengkulu had the potential to produce nutmeg and cloves and it was important that it be run efficiently. Raffles governed the East Indies colony with skill and enthusiasm even though he had to bury three of his four children there: obtaining spices to gratify the home market was a grim job. He went on to found the colony of Singapore where Violet and I cried over the frying chillies, and began the process that turned the strategically located but sparsely populated island into one of the twentieth century's great trading centres.

The East Indies – what we now call Indonesia – is a sprawling archipelago of 13 000 islands and has been perhaps the world's greatest and most consistent source of spices. In their story, the most significant of the islands are the

Overleaf: The lavish use of spices characterizes the cooking of many countries and in India a visit to the spice-seller is an indispensable part of shopping excursions. Europeans and Americans who tend to buy their spices rather more feebly in little glass bottles are unused to the colour and abundance seen in Asian markets.

Moluccas in the east, which produce cloves and nutmeg, and Java and Sumatra in the west, suppliers of pepper to the world. We have no idea when the spice trade began. Cloves from the East Indies have been found in Mesopotamian graves dating from around 3000 BC. They would have had to travel more than 3200 kilometres (2000 miles) by land and sea to get there: an uncertain and terrifying journey at a time when navigation was primitive and roads non-existent. In the Old Testament, when Joseph was stripped of his coat of many colours and sold into slavery by his jealous brothers he was bought by a group of Ishmaelites whose caravan carrying myrrh, balm and gum tragacanth was travelling from Gilead to Egypt. So the trade in spices is an ancient undertaking.

It has always been a profitable one, especially when the spices were destined for Europe. We have already seen how Pliny, like many Romans, complained that his countrymen's taste for pepper was destroying the economy of the empire. The taste for black pepper also captivated the barbarians who destroyed Rome: when Alaric and the Goths laid siege to the city in 408 they demanded 1360 kilograms (3000 pounds) of pepper to spare it. Even after the fall of Rome Europe's hunger for spices could never be satisfied.

It has certainly never been adequately explained. The old truism that spices were in demand to cover up the frightful taste of rotting or rancid ingredients seems absolute nonsense to me. If they were used merely to disguise food that had gone off, why were they so popular in the imperial, royal or aristocratic courts of China, the Arab world and Europe? Courts that could demand and receive supplies of sometimes fresh, and usually superior, ingredients. Nigel Paterson summed up the question of the use of spices with the phrase 'hedonism or necessity'. It seems that hedonism must be the answer: spices brought pleasure and delight to food. Of course, even the grandest in the land must have found their diets tiresome, limited as they were by poor transport, the vagaries of the weather and the need to preserve many foods by salting or drying. Maggie Black has amusingly analysed William the Conqueror's dinner as it is depicted in the Bayeux Tapestry. It starts with pottage, cubed and flat meats and small grilled birds and moves on to 'steaks (entrecotes?), round flatbreads and perhaps chicken pasties. A servitor kneels before William with what may be a dish piled with frumenty (a sort of savoury porridge)'. Another royal meal, given in London by Richard II some 300 years later on 23 September 1387, is even more interesting. The menu features salted beef and fresh beef, salted venison and fresh venison, geese, capons, hens, rabbits, eggs, apples, cream, custards, jellies, pancakes and curiosities like swans, herons, curlews and cranes. Hardly privation, but perhaps lacking in excitement without the use of liberal quantities and varieties of spices.

As we have seen, salt made the boring diet of the poor tolerable. Spices, in a way, merely moved the goalposts by adding titillation to the palatability of the food already gracing lordly tables. Unlike salt, which was more or less for everyone, spices were almost exclusively for the upper echelons of society. As the fourteenth-century millennarian revolutionary John Ball reminds us, the lords 'are clothed in velvet, and warm in their furs, while we go covered with rags. They have wine and spices and fair bread, and we eat oat cake and straw and water to drink.'

Spices certainly brought reputed medical benefits to affluent tables – they were often thought to help ward off the plague, for example – and not only in Europe. Wherever we look magical or medicinal powers are attributed to them. Chinese Taoists thought that cinnamon was a general prophylactic and cloves were considered an aphrodisiac as well as an analgesic; we still use oil of cloves in toothpaste and mouthwash. Arab physicians in medieval Salerno in southern Italy prescribed ginger for ailments of the lungs and kidneys; Indian

Overleaf: In the Middle Ages royal tables – like that of William the Conqueror, shown here in the Bayeux Tapestry – were lavishly supplied with varieties of meat, game and fish, but even this abundance would have been insipid without spices. The old theory that they were added to dishes to conceal the taste of rotting food is probably less to the point than the more up-to-date one that they were used hedonistically to add refinement and extra flavour.

ERVN: PRANDIVM:
E
PO

HIC·EPISCOPVS:CIBV:E
TV: BE NE DIC IT·

doctors used nutmegs to treat freckles, liver disease and madness. Saffron, the only true spice that can be cultivated in Europe, was a celebrated aphrodisiac and was sprinkled on the beds of honeymooners in ancient Rome.

Because spices were so desirable and their trade so zealously guarded, myths sprang up about monsters and devils who guarded them. Herodotus wrote, 'When the Arabians go out to collect cassia [a slightly inferior variety of cinnamon], they cover their bodies and faces, all but their eyes, with oxhides and other skins. The plant grows in a shallow lake which together with the ground around it, is infested by winged creatures like bats which screech alarmingly and are very pugnacious. They have to be kept from attacking the men's eyes while the cassia is being cut.' Fifteen hundred years later the Venetian traveller and trader Marco Polo reported that the overland route to Asia and her spices was 'the abode of many evil spirits which amuse travellers to their destruction with the most extraordinary illusions'. As those who dared were to find out, the real hardships on the spice routes were hazardous enough.

The historical European palate seemed to demand spices with everything as medieval recipes attest. A Norman one for mutton stew, reconstructed by Maggie Black, calls for ginger, cumin and coriander; one for grilled steaks flavours them with ginger and cinnamon; a hare stew requires ginger, mace and cinnamon. And the quantity of spices called for in these recipes was often prodigious. 'Two fourteenth-century Italian recipes, each to serve twelve, call for a base of one half pound of spice,' writes T. Sarah Peterson in her sparkling book *Acquired Taste*. She adds, 'To prepare for a wedding feast for twenty and a supper for ten, one marketing list directs the purchase of a pound and a quarter of ginger, a half pound of cinnamon, an ounce of saffron, a quarter pound of cloves mixed with grains of paradise [coriander], and an eighth of a pound each of long pepper and mace. The grander the occasion and the more one wished to impress, the more spice.' Peterson goes on to propose that in the mid-seventeenth century there was a revolution in European taste, led by French cooks and writers, which resulted in the move away from the centuries-old heavily spiced cuisine to one based on a more limited repertoire of acid, salt flavours that has mostly remained with us. In a way the taste revolution that Peterson described impoverished the European palate. If you wish to be convinced, try some contemporary Middle Eastern or Indian dishes with their extraordinarily complex sweet, savoury and pungent flavourings and you will get a little hint of the tastes our medieval ancestors must have experienced.

There is a lovely passage in Willa Cather's novel *Death Comes for the Archbishop* when a French parish priest is sent to mid-nineteenth century New Mexico to sort out church affairs. He is warmly welcomed by a farming family who kill a young goat in his honour. 'When Father Latour asked her to give him his portion without chili, the girl inquired whether it was more pious to eat it like that. He hastened to explain that Frenchmen as a rule do not like high seasoning . . .' This sentiment is echoed by a French traveller in 1648 whom Peterson quotes as remarking that 'in Germany and in Poland the dishes were so full of saffron and various spices that no Frenchman would be able to eat them.' A sixteenth- or twelfth-century Frenchman, German or Italian would have felt rather differently. Until the mid-seventeenth century the rule was spices with everything and plenty of them. Demand was constant, supply was uncertain and prices were dizzying. Peppercorns were often used to pay taxes, dowries and rents; we still use the expression 'peppercorn' rent. When the remnants of Magellan's fleet limped back to Spain in 1522 after three years at sea in search of a new route to the spice islands, the loss of four ships and the death of Magellan himself as well as most of his crew, the cargo of a little more than one ton of cloves paid for the expedition, gave the king of Spain a substantial profit and made the survivors rich men. Indeed, Juan Sebastian del Cano, who took over command of the expedition after Magellan's death, was granted a commemorative coat of arms emblazoned with twelve cloves, three nutmegs and two cinnamon sticks.

For centuries the trade in spices between Asia and Europe had been

Overleaf: Spices have been used as flavourings for thousands of years, but until comparatively recently they were an expensive luxury destined for the tables of the rich. The poor had to rely almost exclusively on salt to make their food palatable.

controlled by Arab middlemen who knew the secret of the Indian Ocean's monsoon winds – that they blew from Egypt to India in the summer and from India to Egypt throughout the winter and so made trading possible. The Romans also discovered this 'secret', but the spice trade remained an Arab prerogative and Alexandria and Constantinople became great ports of transhipment where the spices passed into the hands of Venetian traders. They also travelled overland to Europe via the miscellany of caravan trails that became known as the Silk Route.

When Marco Polo made his epic journey to China in the thirteenth century he was overwhelmed by the quantity of spices pouring into Imperial China. In the sprawling city of Hangchow he was told – doubtless with some exaggeration – that 5 tons of pepper a day (or nearly 2000 tons a year) entered the city. This was at a time when Europe was consuming something in the order of 1000 tons of pepper a year. The cosy and fabulously profitable relationship between Venice and the Byzantine Empire came to an abrupt end when the Ottoman Turks overran Constantinople in 1453 and disrupted the trade in spices. This has often been cited as the great event that kick-started the Age of Exploration.

Maybe.

I cannot help feeling that Europe hardly needed the trauma of the fall of Constantinople to force it to look outwards. There must have been widespread resentment against Venetian power and its near monopoly of the spice trade. But the monopoly was soon to be a thing of the past: the global shake-up caused by what we call the Age of Exploration signalled the end of Venice's eminence and the disruptive and exciting rise of new maritime powers like Portugal and the Netherlands.

In the fifteenth century the restless, energetic and expansive societies of Castile (which was soon to merge with the crown of Aragon to create Spain) and Portugal were bursting to break the geographical constraints of the Iberian Peninsula. The discovery of the Atlantic islands of Madeira, the Azores and the Canaries were the first tentative steps into a wider, newer world. Marco Polo's descriptions of Asian wealth were vivid, tantalizing and reinforced by other travellers' accounts as well as by mere hearsay. The pressures to get to Asia were building up. They were chiefly commercial – and gastronomic – but given a philosophical gloss by the wish to trounce the Arabs and spread the gospel throughout 'heathen' Asia.

The earth was generally known – amongst the intelligentsia – to be round and the search for an all-sea route to the East was starting. The Portuguese would logically and successfully go down the coast of Africa, around the Cape of Good Hope and across the Indian Ocean; the Spanish, thanks to Columbus' daring and brilliance, would go west and find America in their way.

The explorers and their masters were hard and canny men. That their motivation was cash or glory rather than the expansion of human knowledge does not make their achievements any less substantial nor their impact on the rest of the world any less fatal. For our purposes I cannot overstate the fact that it was chiefly – indeed almost exclusively – Europe's taste for pepper, cinnamon, cloves and other spices that changed the face of the world for ever.

The rise of Portugal is perhaps the most instructive to modern minds. Accustomed as we are to seeing it as a pleasant holiday destination – thanks to a mild climate, friendly people and low prices – and one of Western Europe's poorest countries, it is difficult to think of it as one of the first great global superpowers. Geography helped: a long Atlantic-facing coastline made the Portuguese good sailors and skilful fishermen. And so did a major breakthrough in ship design. As Braudel explains, the birth in about 1430 of the

Overleaf: The demand for spices to add colour and interest to the often monotonous diets of our ancestors was so great that obtaining and selling them was often a matter of government policy. They were a major force in creating the great global empires that changed the world: the rise and fall of Portugal, Spain and the Netherlands was intimately bound up with the search for them; and some of the greatest human adventures, like Magellan's round-the-world voyage, were the result of our wish to have spices on our tables.

Portuguese caravel was a great leap forward. She combined the square sail of the North with the lateen or triangular sail of the Mediterranean and these adaptable sails, sturdy clinker-built hull and centrally mounted rudder made her the first European ship that could undertake major ocean voyages with reasonable reliability and confidence. Prince Henry the Navigator encouraged Portuguese maritime skill through the establishment of an informal 'school' of navigation and geography based around his court at Sagres in the Algarve and introduced massive state intervention into the hitherto rather private business of trade and exploration.

Henry died in 1460 but his policies bore fruit posthumously, first when Bartholomew Dias reached the Cape of Good Hope in 1487 and more significantly when Vasco da Gama and his fleet reached Calicut, India's greatest spice port, in 1498. Events unfolded explosively. Within 15 years the Portuguese Empire girdled the world from Sumatra to Brazil and oriental spices began to pour into Lisbon – the new Venice, as it were.

The expansion of Spanish power had proceeded apace with that of the Portuguese, but Spain fared less well in the race to control the world's spices. The 'New World' of Columbus and his successors had less to offer in terms of spices than the Asian Old World so effectively seized by the Portuguese, and the Spanish, preoccupied as they were with the Americas, never really succeeded in establishing themselves in the East until they finally took control of the rather less valuable Philippines in about 1570.

The race between the monarchies of Spain and Portugal to exploit the world and its spices led to the bizarre moment when Pope Alexander VI divided the world between the Iberian countries. Alexander was a Spaniard and wanted Spain to support his territorial ambitions for his illegitimate son in Italy. Ferdinand and Isabella, the reigning Spanish monarchs, were pressing him to recognize Spanish claims to the new lands that Columbus had visited on his first voyage. The pope was compliant and issued a series of bulls recognizing Spain's sovereignty of the West Indies. Eventually he decreed that everything on the other side of an imaginary line 100 leagues to the west of the Azores would belong to Spain. John II of Portugal, who knew that the Portuguese were heading in the right direction for Asian spices when they travelled east, accepted the papal line as a starting point for negotiations with Spain. He only asked for the line to be moved another 270 leagues to the west. As J. H. Parry explains in *The Spanish Seaborne Empire*, 'The Spanish Monarchs, secure in the delusions which Columbus had fostered about the Western route to Asia, agreed . . . The Treaty of Tordesillas was duly signed in April 1494, a diplomatic triumph for Portugal, confirming to the Portuguese not only the true route to India but most of the South Atlantic.' Portugal's imperial aspirations turned out to be a poisoned chalice: a marginal power thrust into the limelight of the world stage by an over-achieving monarchy was doomed to failure. 'To control this far flung Empire, thousands of young men sailed every year from Portugal. Few were to return, which was an enormous drain on the country's manpower,' Joanna Hall Brierly remarks in her skilful history of the Indonesian spice trade. 'Many would die on the long voyage. Others would be killed in battles at sea, some would desert, while large numbers would be decimated by disease – malaria, dysentery and fevers.' As Brierly notes, Portugal could not sustain a big enough navy to secure her scattered empire and came to depend increasingly on unreliable and expensive mercenary sailors. The highwater mark of Portuguese power was relatively fleeting. Within less than a century Portugal had become one of the great has-beens of history.

As Portugal's Asian empire sickened and died two little nations from the hitherto neglected and out-of-the-way north-west corner of Europe flung themselves on the corpse like savage and tenacious terriers. They were England and the Netherlands, newly emerging commercial buccaneers determined to have their place in the sun. By the beginning of the seventeenth century Dutch and English traders were starting to make inroads into the lucrative Spice Islands trade. The East India Company was chartered in London in 1600 and in 1602 the rival United East India Company was established in Amsterdam. Both companies were powerful trading and naval entities and gradually developed into states within states, making war, negotiating treaties and eventually governing tracts of land far more extensive than their native countries. With better ships than the Portuguese who had failed to keep up with changes in naval technology and were still relying on the once revolutionary but now rather dated caravel – and more potent commercial interests behind them, the companies established trading footholds in the east. The Dutch were at first more successful than the English but commercial rivalry resulted in the Anglo-Dutch Wars of 1652–55, 1665–67, 1672–78 and 1680–84. These years of warfare left a bitter legacy in the English language which is still studded with mildly derogatory anti-Dutch expressions: 'Dutch uncle', 'Dutch courage' and 'going Dutch'.

The causes and consequences of Dutch colonial success in Asia raise interesting historical problems, chiefly the question of national character and how it changes. What are the Dutch like today? Tolerant, liberal, kind and humane are some of the words we would use to characterize them. And they created a great civilization throughout the seventeenth century in an astonishing creative outburst as they won their independence from the Spanish Habsburgs. Seventeenth-century Holland is one of the first recognizably modern societies: clean, cosy and prosperous. The legacy of that society remains tangible not just in the neat, pretty houses and canals of Amsterdam but, more significantly, in the paintings of Rembrandt, Ter Borch, Tenniers, Van Ruysdael and Vermeer that adorn museums around the world. Amsterdam was one of the world's great metropolises, doubling its population during the century and bursting with civic pride and innovation. It was, for example, the first city to have street lights and a professionally organized fire brigade. This flowering of Dutch civilization was fertilized by trade – and mostly by the lucrative spice trade from the newly acquired colonies in the East Indies. There the picture becomes less pretty: Dutch enterprise in the Spice Islands was heartless and authoritarian, teetering on the brink of sadism.

In 1618 Jan Pieterszoon Coen, an accountant turned imperialist, became

Spices were among the first commodities to be bought and sold internationally. The trade in foodstuffs ranging from spices to grain was an early sign of our shrinking world and the creation of the global economy.

AM.USH .... AM.USH USH
1019.00 92-25 1020.00 92-26 92-25

governor-general of the Dutch East Indies. His policy was to do anything that would secure Dutch commercial interests in the spice trade. From his newly-conquered capital Batavia (present day Jakarta), he launched an expedition against the Banda Islands, source of nutmeg. Forty-four people were killed and the remaining islanders fled or were sold into slavery. Coen set up Dutch adventurers as nutmeg planters in their place. One of the Banda Islands, Pulo Run, remained under nominal English sovereignty, an anomaly resolved by the treaty of Breda in 1665 when it was ceded to the Dutch in a bout of territorial swaps that compensated the English with the then much less significant island of Manhattan. To keep the price of spices high, Coen and his successors ruthlessly controlled their production: seventy war canoes swept the islands of the Indonesian archipelago destroying unauthorized clove and nutmeg plantations. 'This was particularly cruel,' Brierly tells us, 'as it was a Moluccan tradition to plant a clove tree for the birth of a child. Conversely, destroying a tree was meant to foretell doom for the child. On Tidore and Ternate, the original home of the clove, production had been the sole income for the islanders. The penalty for cultivating extra spices was death.'

The Dutch policy of destroying trees and meting out savage punishment to offenders carried on until the early nineteenth century, bringing poverty and misery to the islands. But this poverty and misery brought rivers of gold to the coffers of the United East India Company. European consumers either did not know or did not care that their nutmeg, cloves and precious black pepper were watered with blood and tears. English policy towards the East Indies was less violently single-minded than that of the Dutch and the East India Company concentrated most of its activities in India.

In spite of their draconian policy, the near monopoly on spices enjoyed by the Dutch began to slip away from them. In a stunning act of agricultural espionage the Frenchman Pierre Poivre (aptly named for a notable in the history of spices – *poivre* is French for pepper) managed to smuggle cloves out of the Indies to Mauritius in the early 1770s. From there they were introduced to Zanzibar in 1818 and by the end of the century the island was producing three-quarters of the world's clove supplies. Ironically, Indonesia (which incorporates the old Spice Islands) is now the world's biggest importer of cloves. Instead of finding their way on to the table they go up in smoke as an indispensable ingredient in *kretek* cigarettes.

Nutmegs also emigrated: production was successfully established in the British controlled West Indies. But although sources of supply had been diversified, the most sought after spices remained expensive and difficult to obtain and trading profits consequently remained high. In the first half of the nineteenth century American spice traders – mostly based in Salem, Massachusetts – could count on profits of around 700 per cent for every cargo of black pepper they brought back to America.

Today the great age of spices is passing as other products crowd the markets of the world. This is not a new phenomenon. As Braudel has pointed out, the percentage of spices as part of world trade started falling in the eighteenth century as growing and transporting them became less susceptible to the vagaries of politics, piracy or war. By the beginning of the twentieth century spices had become rather ordinary.

But spice production remains highly concentrated and surprisingly precarious. In 1955 Hurricane Janet savaged the West Indies. Grenada was particularly hard hit and in a matter of a few hours nearly half of the world's nutmeg supply was destroyed.

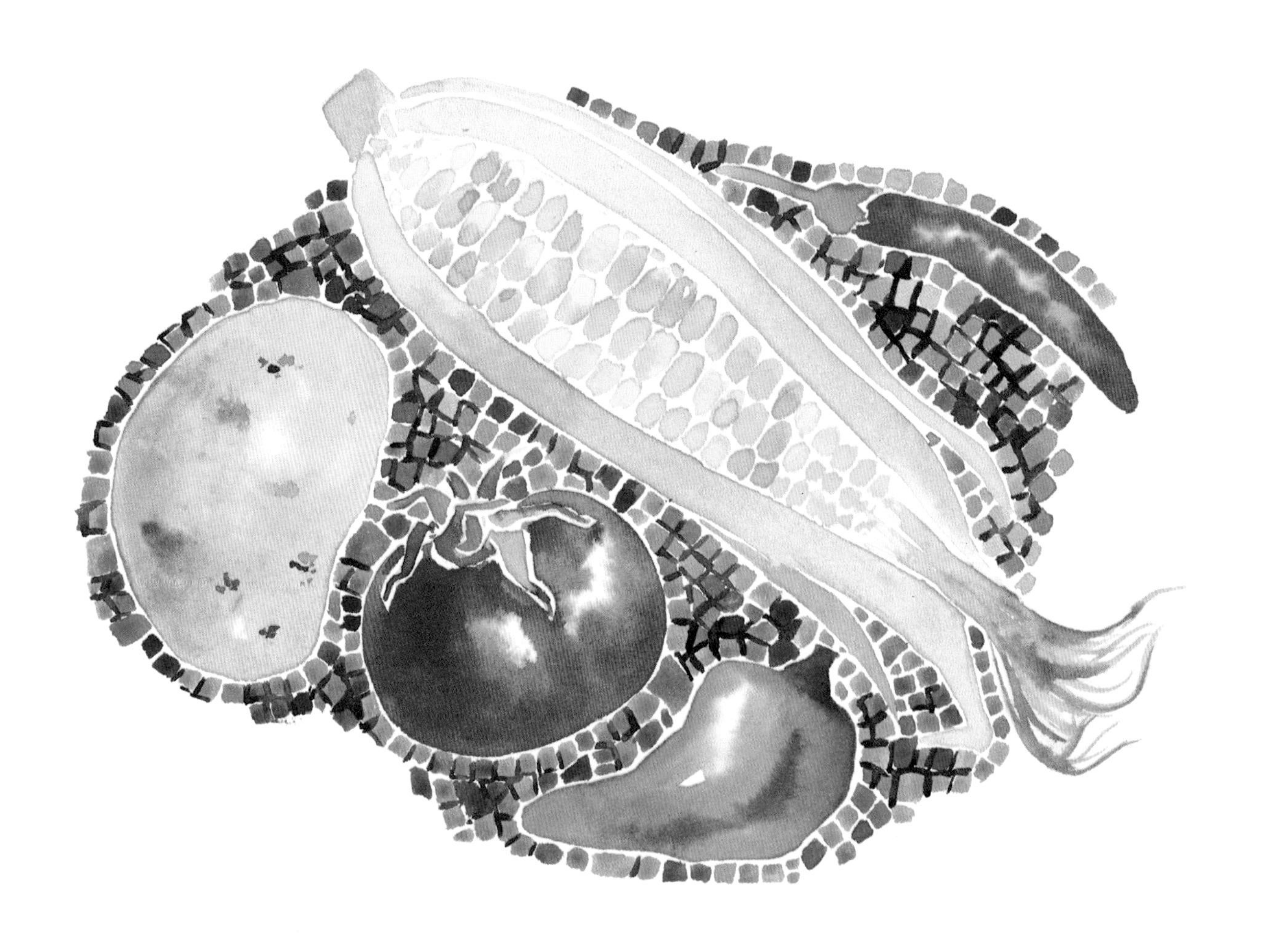

Montezuma's Legacy

East of Naples the volcanic ash from successive eruptions of Mount Vesuvius has settled to create immensely fertile land ideally suited for the cultivation of tomatoes, particularly the sweet, juicy and plum-shaped San Marzano variety which is squashed into purée or put into cans found on grocers' shelves in every corner of the earth. I visited a relatively small – 10 hectares (about five acres) – farm there owned by the Longobardi family. Signora Longobardi gently fried some chopped garlic and onion in olive oil and then added a little red chilli pepper and a few pounds of tomatoes to make a sauce for the family's spaghetti supper: a supper they and thousands of other Italian families eat almost every evening. Signor Longobardi took me on a tour of the farm to look at the big polythene tunnels where the red chillies are grown in temperatures that climb to 50°C (122°F) at midday and to admire his fields of tomatoes ripening on the vine. The Longobardis grow about a quarter of a million pounds (nearly 113 500 kilograms) of tomatoes a year and from the middle of their farm there are tomato fields as far as the eye can see. Tomato farm after tomato farm flourishes in the area, all thanks to the hot Mediterranean sun of southern Italy and the volcanic ash of Vesuvius, beautiful, threatening and looming on the horizon. As Anna del Conte writes in her magisterial *Gastronomy of Italy*, 'The uses of tomatoes in Italian cooking are endless. They are made into sauces to dress pasta, gnocchi and *riso*, they are added to other food for flavouring, they are eaten in salads, stewed with other vegetables as in *peperonata* and stuffed in many ways.' Throughout Italy, but in the south in particular, the tomato is the king of the Italian kitchen. It is hard indeed to picture Italian food without tomatoes. Harder still, perhaps, to realize that their introduction into Italian cooking is a relatively recent innovation that began in the eighteenth century when they first found their way into recipes in Italy and gathered momentum as those recipes were recorded and popularized by cookery writers. The flood tide of Italian tomatoes started flowing in the late nineteenth century when the development of canning and concentrating processes began making tomatoes available to Italian cooks everywhere, all year. Italian cooking without tomatoes? Unthinkable, absurd, impossible – but fact until modern times.

The *Larousse Gastronomique* underlines the tomato's central role in national and regional kitchens: 'Iberian, Italian, Basque and Languedocian cookery are unimaginable without the tomato, and it is also used in the cookery of most other European countries, including Hungary and Britain. The tomato is also indispensable in classic French cooking.' It is a curious fact that the tomato, for all its deliciousness and versatility, was greeted with fear and derision when it left its Central American homeland as a hopeful traveller. It was grown as a botanical curiosity, but no one dared eat it: after all, it was *poisonous.*

In September 1820 a large and excited crowd gathered outside the Court House, the most imposing building in the small town of Salem, New Jersey. Forty-nine-year-old Colonel Robert Gibbons Johnson, local bigwig and gentleman farmer, was the man people had come to see. Hundreds had travelled from miles around because the colonel was going to defy death – by eating a tomato. In a radio dramatization of the event, broadcast in 1949, Johnson turns to the crowd and says, 'What are you afraid of? Being poisoned? Well I'm not and I'll show you fools that these things are good to eat.' He ate the tomato and lived and Salem, New Jersey, became the centre of a thriving tomato-growing industry. The town has staged a tomato festival centred around Robert Gibbon Johnson Day since 1988. People descend on Salem to play games with tomatoes, eat tomatoes and have tomatoes painted on their faces. And the local theatre company re-enacts the famous tomato-eating scene. It is all rather marvellous and good fun. Except for one thing. According to Andrew Smith, tomato historian *par excellence*, the colonel never ate a tomato in public to prove its wholesomeness. Smith notes that, 'The Johnson story could be dismissed as simply a good old yarn that accidentally became a national legend, but it is not the only tomato introduction story.' He has recorded 500 stories about the first tomato-eater in America alone, ranging from Thomas Jefferson to an anonymous black slave to a Shaker bride in Mount Lebanon, New York.

The origins of tomato-eating in its adopted homelands from America to Italy are shrouded in myth and mystery. Why the tomato? The glib answer could be that until the advent of marketing and advertising human taste in food had always been extremely conservative. But the tomato spread at a time when an array of new foods was entering our diets. The answer must lie in the fact that the tomato is a very unusual product. It is a fruit, but we eat it like a vegetable. Renaissance herbalists classified the first tomatoes they encountered alongside the mandrake and its more poisonous cousin, the deadly nightshade. Because the mandrake's roots are said to resemble a man and woman locked in a passionate embrace, it and its relatives were credited with aphrodisiacal qualities, hence early names for the tomato include *poma amoris* and *pomme d'amour* and their translation, love apple. The relationship with deadly nightshade, and the fruit's rather high acidity, led to fears that it was poisonous.

Although Europeans must have eaten and enjoyed tomatoes – it was known that they were used for sauces in their Central American homeland – they remained a minority taste in many places. Writing about her late Victorian childhood in *Lark Rise to Candleford*, Flora Thompson describes how her fictional self (Laura) asked a pedlar for a love apple: '"You don't want any o' they," the pedlar tells her. "Nasty, sour things they be, as only the gentry can eat. You have a nice sweet orange wi' your penny." But Laura felt she must taste the love apples and insisted upon having one. Such daring created quite a sensation among the onlookers. '"Don't 'ee go tryin' to eat it now,"' one woman urged. "It'll only make 'ee sick. I know because I had one of the nasty, horrid things at our Minnie's"' Our love affair with the tomato was a slow burner, kindled in the sixteenth century and taking 300 years to get roaring.

Brandi
La grande
della pizza!!

Who knows which heroic individual ate the first tomato? I do not feel that food history needs always to rely on the Great Man theory in which every innovation is the result of the action of some larger-than-life individual like Colonel Johnson, the mythical 'first' tomato eater in America. But the story of the tomato, the potato, maize, and all the other rather bizarre and grudgingly accepted products of the New World which have risen to culinary glory almost everywhere, owes much to a great man whom we skirted round in the last chapter: Christopher Columbus. Attempts to commemorate the 500th anniversary of his first voyage of 1492 foundered on reefs of more than just fashionable political correctness. Many people felt strongly that much of the Columbus effect – the destruction, enslavement or degradation of the native peoples of the Americas – should be condemned rather than celebrated.

Columbus was not just an individual, but a type: one of many ruthless, brave, arrogant fifteenth-century Mediterranean hustlers who made the Age of Exploration happen. If he had not reached the West Indies someone else would have done so, with the same tragic and enthralling consequences. But Columbus got there first and, for better or worse, is one of the very few people whose vision, egotism and pigheadedness forever changed the course of history. Certainly, no single individual so changed the way the world eats. And it was all by accident. The son of a Genoese weaver and petty entrepreneur, Columbus sailed the trade routes of the Mediterranean and the European Atlantic, married into the minor nobility (his father-in-law did well out of the Portuguese settlement of the Azores) and developed his plans for reaching the riches of the Indies by sailing westwards. He hawked himself unsuccessfully to the courts of Portugal, France and England and was saved from oblivion by the lukewarm interest of the Spanish monarchs Ferdinand and Isabella. Portuguese success in sailing down the African coast was making Spain's rulers

The ancestors of the pizza stretch back to Roman times, but the dish that we know today would be unthinkable without the addition of a brash immigrant from South America: the tomato.

nervous and their gradual reconquest of Moorish-occupied Spain (which was complete in 1492) meant that they no longer received tribute money from their former Muslim subjects. So the Columbus gamble was worth taking. According to the historian Felipe Fernández-Armesto, equipping the expedition cost about as much as 'the annual income of a middling provincial aristocrat'.

Success would bring treasure and increased status to the Spanish monarchy. The rewards to Columbus were relatively greater. The Genoese weaver's son would get one-tenth of all the profits from his enterprise and – just as important for his vainglory – the hereditary titles of admiral, viceroy and governor. As Fernández-Armesto remarks, 'The effect, one could suggest, was to turn the Ocean Sea and all its lands into a potential feudal seigneury only a short way removed from a principality.'

As we know the gamble paid off: but in a way that none of the participants, least of all Columbus himself, expected.

The explorer underestimated the circumference of the earth by about a fifth – neither the spices of India nor the silks of China were as close to Spain as he thought – and the Americas were in the way. So Columbus began his voyage in error. But he did make the profound decision, based on either knowledge or intuition, to use the powerful oceanic wind systems that blew across the Atlantic in different directions. In the past sailors had often sailed against the wind when they left port: slow going to their destination but at least a guarantee that they would be able to return.

Columbus, by travelling south before turning west, found what came to be known as the trade winds which blow across the Atlantic from Africa to the Caribbean. On the way home he was able to take advantage of the westerlies which blow from America to Europe. Just as the monsoon winds of the Indian Ocean allowed the spice trade with the East to develop, this powerful combination of trade winds and westerlies made regular transport and communications between the Old World and the New possible.

So Columbus sailed west and made landfall on what is now Watling Island in the Bahamas on 12 October 1492. He later sighted Cuba and reached

Hispaniola (modern Haiti and the Dominican Republic). The voyage was a success. Except for one minor detail: they had not reached China or India, or even the mythical island of Cipangu. And there were no spices. Or at least none that Columbus recognized. No nutmeg, cloves or cinnamon. No black pepper. But explorers – especially explorers who are hoping to make a fortune for themselves and their patrons – are optimists. 'I simply do not know where to go next,' Columbus wrote, 'I never tire from looking at such luxurious vegetation, which is so different from ours. I believe that there are many plants and trees here that could be worth a lot in Spain for use as dyes, spices and medicines, but to my great sorrow I do not recognize them.' He was overwhelmed and puzzled by what he saw. He writes again that, 'This island of Isabella may have many valuable spices, but I do not recognize them and this causes me a great deal of sorrow for I see a thousand kinds of fruit trees, each of which is green now as in Spain during the months of May and June; there are also a thousand kinds of plants and herbs and the same with flowers.' Wherever Columbus looked there was fertility, abundance and wonder, but nothing familiar or recognizable. The 'admiral of the ocean sea' was positively reeling from the shock of the new. He struggled to describe the native Indian foodstuffs. Sweet potatoes, he reported, looked like carrots and tasted like chestnuts; he more accurately recorded that chillies are 'their pepper' and added hopefully that they were 'worth more than our pepper; no one eats without them, because it is very healthy.'

Nonetheless, the Spaniards shunned the native food. After describing the fruit and vegetable staples of the Indian diet, Chanca, the physician on Columbus' second voyage, notes that the islands' inhabitants cooked chillies with whatever fish and birds they could catch and that, 'They have some nuts

Overleaf: Chillies were one of the many exotic foodstuffs that Columbus discovered in the West Indies, where they grew in profusion. They have emigrated since then and are used in cooking throughout the world – particularly in the cuisines of South-east Asia and India.

like hazels, very good to eat. They eat any snakes, lizards or spiders and worms that they find on the ground, and their habits seem to be more bestial than those of any beasts in the world.' The Spaniards thought it was hardly a diet fit for Christians and when a settlement was established on Hispaniola in 1494 European plants and animals were imported to supplement the local produce.

The settlement failed painfully, tragically, dismally and food was chief among the causes of that failure. 'Columbus's assumption that the Spaniards would forego wheaten bread in favour of the local sort, made from cassava, is revealing of the essentially cultural problems which colonization posed,' Fernández-Armesto observes. 'A native diet was deficient in protein in comparison with Spanish custom. To satisfy hunger from native food, Spaniards had to eat enormous quantities which defied the capacity of the local economy, geared to subsistence or very small surpluses.' Ironically, in the midst of tropical abundance, food was a persistent problem with early Spanish settlements in the Americas. As J. H. Parry notes, these new 'Spanish towns insistently demanded wheat flour, wine and oil. All could be imported, but at very high prices.'

Columbus failed to plant a flourishing colony; he failed to convert the natives to Christianity and killed most of them instead; he failed to reach Asia; and he failed to find any spices or very much gold. But he began to open a new world of food to mankind and profoundly changed the diet of hundreds of millions of people. It was the greatest accident in history. As A. V. Crosby has pointed out, the Indians of the Americas developed the cultivation of maize, guavas, beans, avocados, peanuts, pineapples, pumpkins, papayas, potatoes, tomatoes and chilli peppers. We eat the consequences of Columbus' voyages every day.

His success encouraged other wannabe lords and aspiring millionaires, tough men bred in the rough and tumble of newly united Spain who were ready to risk their lives – and the lives of their mostly riff-raff followers – crossing the world, looking for action. Like Columbus they were amazed and bewildered by the novelty of the world they were exploring, particularly when they first came into contact with the rich, complex and highly developed civilizations of the mainland. When Hernando Cortés and his men marched through Mexico in 1519 they were dazzled by the abundance of foodstuffs. 'When we arrived at the great marketplace,' Cortés' companion and chronicler Bernal Diaz del Castillo reports, 'we were astounded at the number of people and the quantity of merchandise that it contained . . . Let us go on and speak of those who sold beans and sage and other vegetables and herbs in another part, and to those who sold fowls, cocks with wattles, rabbits, hares, deer, mallards, young dogs and other things of that sort in their part of the market and let us also mention the fruiterers, and the women who sold cooked food, dough and tripe in their own part of the market.'

Montezuma, the Aztec emperor, ruled his Mexico-wide empire from the city of Tenochtitlan, a grander city than any in sixteenth-century Europe. Teams of chefs offered him meals that consisted of thirty different dishes. 'I have heard it said,' del Castillo writes, 'that they were wont to cook him the flesh of young boys, but as he had such a variety of dishes, made of so many things, we could not succeed in seeing if they were of human flesh or other things.' The emperor dined on turkey, pheasant, wild duck, boar, venison, partridges and rabbit, all accompanied by the *tortilla* bread that remains an indispensable part of Mexican eating, and, 'as soon as he began to eat they placed before him a sort of wooden screen painted over with gold, so that no one should watch him eating.'

Among the many edible wonders encountered by Cortés and his conquistadores was a smooth-skinned red fruit known as the *xitomatl*, which was soon to begin its incredible journey from the markets of Montezuma's empire to

Overleaf: Mexican food is still based on ingredients that would have been familiar to the Aztecs: maize, beans, chillies and tomatoes. Indeed, we know from Spanish accounts of the conquest of Mexico that Montezuma enjoyed his *tortillas* but that, as an emperor, he ate them behind a golden screen, protected from his courtiers' gaze.

the kitchens of Naples. And everywhere they looked, from the emperor's table to the poorest household, they saw *tortillas* and *tamales* made from maize. Although maize was one of the first plants that Columbus observed in the New World and brought back to Europe it was only when Europeans encountered the much more densely populated and advanced Aztec and Inca cultures that its real potential as a foodstuff could be appreciated. Indeed, as J. H. Parry has explained, the Aztec dependency on the plant helped to create their empire. Maize could sustain dense populations, but as land became exhausted more land on which to grow it had to be found. The Aztec dilemma was stark: conquer or starve. In the words of John Collier, maize 'brought about the change from wandering to settled life and the possibility of such populations as those estimated for the Inca Empire at its height – ten to sixteen million . . .' Without it the great civilizations of the New World 'could not have come into existence'.

Maize is a fantastically prolific crop: at least three times as productive as wheat, it is able to grow on 3600 metre (12 000 ft) Andean peaks, or in arid deserts or humid jungles. We know that it was domesticated about 5000 BC, probably in Mexico from where it spread throughout the Americas. But we cannot know for certain how the domesticated plant developed. Uniquely, it is unable to reproduce itself without human help: the kernels that we eat – the seeds of the plant – are so tightly imprisoned within the tough outer husk that they would be strangled as they sprouted unless someone took them out and planted them. It cannot exist without man: it is the plant world's equivalent of the domesticated dog, locked forever in an intimate relationship with another species. Maize cultivation spread relatively quickly throughout Mediterranean Europe. It was growing in Spain in the 1520s and inhabitants of north-eastern Italy were quick to use this abundant new grain in their *polenta* – a sort of porridge that had traditionally been made from spelt, millet or buckwheat.

The development of the slave trade, which is described in the next chapter, also encouraged the cultivation of maize in Portugal's African colonies where the grain was first used as cheap and dependable food for the slave voyage to

America, then developed into a staple for much of Africa. Maize had even spread to China by the end of the sixteenth century.

Today it is the third most important crop in the world but, ironically, its place at the table is hardly obvious. In Central and South America it retains its historic primacy – it provides nearly 40 per cent of the energy in the Mexican diet – and it is the staple food in many desperately poor African countries, but even in corn crazy America only about 2 per cent of food energy comes directly from it. So where do the millions and millions of tons of maize that are cultivated go?

Writing in *National Geographic*, anthropologist Robert Rhoades describes a typical American day: 'You put on a cotton shirt which has fibres strengthened by corn starch. The eggs you eat for breakfast were laid by a corn-fed chicken. At lunch you drink a cold cola sweetened with corn syrup. In the afternoon you read a *National Geographic* – the paper fibres are bound with corn starch to keep them together as they race through high-speed presses. You drive home in a car powered, in part, by ethanol, a fuel derived from corn. When you get there, you feed your dog pet food containing corn meal. You mix yourself a Manhattan with bourbon distilled from corn. For dinner you eat a steak that was once a steer fattened on corn feed. You take out the garbage in a trash bag derived from corn. Finally you brush your teeth with toothpaste containing traces of sorbitol, a sweet powder processed from corn to make the paste tasty.' Even without cornflakes, corn on the cob or popcorn, corn is always on the menu.

The Spanish conquerors of America failed to grasp the significance of its native foodstuffs. They regarded them mostly as botanical curiosities for others to develop and possibly exploit. Their exploitation of American resources was rather more crude: plunder not plants motivated them. Famously, they enslaved the people of Peru and forced them to work in the gold mines rather than till their fields. In 1781 rebellious Indians demonstrated the relative values of gold and corn by forcing a Spanish governor, Don Antonio Arriaga, to make a meal of molten gold. Arriaga's fatal meal reminds us that while the gold and silver of the Americas was most immediately attractive to the Spanish and

Portuguese, it was the food of the New World that was to have a much more profound effect on our lives.

While maize was welcomed and cultivated widely and relatively quickly beyond the Americas, one of the continent's other great foodstuffs was the object of the same fear and loathing as the tomato. This edible hate object was the potato.

Like tomatoes, potatoes are members of the *Solanum* family which includes aubergines and chilli peppers, ornamentals like petunias, tobacco and, of course, the toxic nightshades. As the Spaniards pressed into South America under the leadership of Francisco Pizarro they collided with another vast, authoritarian empire – that of the Inca – which was centred around Peru and Ecuador but stretched as far as north-western Argentina. The Inca had begun cultivating potatoes somewhere in the Peruvian Andes, possibly some 7000 years ago, at about the same time that corn was first domesticated. Both foodstuffs share a relative indifference to geographical and climatic extremes and are exceptionally high yielding and potatoes could support fairly large populations in the unpromising conditions of the Andes. Perhaps unsurprisingly, in the rush to rape the Inca treasury, Pizarro and his troops failed to take note of the tuber that had helped to build the empire they were so bloodily dismembering. (It must be said that of all conquistadores Pizarro, an illiterate, illegitimate peasant who disgracefully murdered the Inca emperor Atahualpa through a rigged trial, was perhaps the most single-minded. His conquest of the huge Inca empire with an army of 180 men and twenty-seven horses is one of the great David and Goliath moments of history.) However, potatoes were observed soon after his conquest and Pedro Cieza de Leon wrote in 1553 that, 'Besides maize, there are two other products which form the principal food of

Diego Rivera's powerful and radical murals of Mexican life before the Spanish Conquest give native crops like maize a starring role. The discovery and diffusion of New World plants caused the single greatest change in human diets since the development of agriculture.

these Indians. One is called Potato and is a kind of earth nut, which after it has been boiled, is as tender as a cooked chestnut, but it has no more skin than a truffle and it grows under the earth in the same way.' Not long afterwards potatoes arrived in Spain – they were on sale in Seville market by 1573 – and received the usual treatment for New World plants, first being grown in a few botanical gardens as curiosities then slowly winning acceptance as a crop. Romantic tales of Sir Walter Raleigh or Sir Francis Drake introducing them to Europe are sadly untrue, but early in the seventeenth century Raleigh may have taken the fateful step of bringing potato cultivation to Ireland.

In spite of the ease with which they can grow and their colossal yields, potatoes were grudgingly accepted and then only by the most desperate members of the European peasantry. Early in the eighteenth century, the 'enlightened' despot Frederick William I of Prussia ordered his peasants to plant and grow them, threatening that those who failed to follow the royal suggestion would have their noses sliced off. The enforced cultivation of potatoes gave Prussia a thriving and well-fed if brutalized peasantry – a fact that was observed and copied by other German states. In 1757, during the Seven Years War, a twenty-year-old French soldier was captured and sent to Westphalia as a prisoner of war. He survived largely on a diet of potatoes just like the local farmers. Years later Antoine Augustin Parmentier became chief pharmacist at Les Invalides, the sumptuous baroque home and hospital for old soldiers in Paris. However, scandal blotted his career: he was forced to resign over allegations that he had made the old soldiers eat 'pig food' – potatoes. But France was densely populated and subject to periodic famines and Parmentier was determined to make the potato France's national vegetable and the country's most reliable foodstuff.

In 1779 he won a competition for 'plants that can replace cereals in time of famine' and continued his crusade, strongly supported by the celebrated chemist Antoine Lavoisier (who discovered the importance of oxygen), the philosopher, wit and man of letters Voltaire, and Benjamin Franklin, revolutionary America's ambassador to the court of Louis XVI. The king himself began to wear a buttonhole of potato flowers and Parmentier organized lavish banquets at which the vegetable featured in every course. Most cannily, he arranged for his experimental potato patch near Les Invalides to be ostentatiously guarded by soldiers in order to create the impression that the crop was especially valuable. All went according to plan: thieves pilfered the potatoes and they started to be grown throughout France. The potato rapidly became a French national staple and French fried potatoes began their climb to world-wide popularity. By the early 1800s the United States president Thomas Jefferson was serving them at White House dinners. Parmentier, the apostle of the potato, remains a familiar figure to 50 million Frenchmen, memorialized in dishes like *potage Parmentier* (potato soup) and *hachis Parmentier*, the French answer to shepherd's pie.

By the time Parmentier died in 1813 the high-yielding potato was on its way to becoming the staple food of millions of people throughout Europe. Nutritious, quick-growing and easy to cultivate, it helped to create the huge populations that were the workforce for the spreading Industrial Revolution. But over-reliance on this single crop presented Europe with a human tragedy that has only been superseded by the Holocaust. In 1845 a mysterious disease began to affect potatoes in Belgium, France, Germany, the Netherlands and Switzerland. Healthy vegetables rotted, turned black and became inedible. The disease – potato blight, caused by the fungus *Phytophtora infestans* – struck Ireland in September 1845. 'We stop the Press with very great regret,' the *Gardener's Chronicle* wrote, 'to announce that the potato Murrain has unequivocally declared itself in Ireland.'

The *Chronicle* went on to ask a life or death question. 'Where will Ireland be in the event of a universal potato rot?'

Overleaf: A street seller in La Paz, Bolivia, presents a dazzling array of different types of potato: in its Andean homelands the vegetable remains a subject for connoisseurship. There are about 4000 species and different types of potato are used for different purposes: baking, boiling and even freeze-drying.

Where indeed? Ireland was more dependent on potato cultivation than any other country in Europe. Although grain was grown there it was an export crop to earn cash for landlords. A population explosion – from three million in 1800 to eight million in 1845 – had been fuelled by reliable supplies of cheap potatoes. The tenancy system created by largely absentee English landlords encouraged uneconomically small farms but a smallholding could produce enough potatoes to feed a large Irish family. Any that the family did not eat were fed to pigs and chickens. Towards the middle of the nineteenth century the average adult Irishman was eating 5.5 kilograms (12 pounds) of the vegetable every day. Potato blight brutally upset the demographic balancing act that had allowed a country of such scanty resources to support such a swollen population. Ireland was in torment for four years as the disease struck again and again: crop failures and starvation brought fever in their wake. Who knows how many died? Certainly one million; maybe 1½ million. A million Irish emigrated and emigration became a fact of life in post-famine Ireland: four million more people left the country in the years up to 1910, creating huge Irish populations in England and the United States. Ireland was changed forever. It became a sparsely populated exporter of people; and its relationship with England, whose relief efforts had been inadequate, was embittered. Potato cultivation returned to Ireland after the famine, and the vegetable is still highly esteemed by the Irish, but the country has never again depended on one crop – even when that crop is the 'reliable' potato.

In its Andean birthplace it is still exalted beyond all other plants. In the mountains of Peru a potato is not just a potato. (There are, by the way, about 4000 varieties.) Each type has its name, characteristics and uses. One will do for supper, but not for lunch. Another is best for breakfast. Some are for boiling and some for baking. Others are used for *chuno*, an ancient freeze-drying technique that preserves potatoes and protects against the consequences of disease and drought. Peruvian farmers also hedge their bets by planting as many as fifty different kinds of potato, a legacy from the Inca who regularly cultivated more varieties of crops than any other ancient peoples, secure in the knowledge that this provided them with an agricultural insurance policy. Such inter-cropping decreases the likelihood of catastrophic disease and helps guard against soil exhaustion.

New types of potato are being uncovered all the time in the Andean wilderness, mainly by Carlos Ochoa, a seventy-three-year-old plant-hunter celebrated as the Indiana Jones of the potato world. The search for new varieties is not just an exercise in botanical vanity. Potatoes found growing in the wild may have greater resistance to drought and disease or may be even more nutritious than commonly grown species. The potato will continue to feed the world: 75 per cent of people live in the ninety-five developing countries that grow potatoes. Better potatoes can mean better lives.

Bitter Sweet

CHAPTER 7

In the 1950s America was in love with Hawaii. Brave little Hawaii, cruelly bashed by the Japanese sneak attack on Pearl Harbour on 7 December 1941 which kicked off World War II in the Pacific; exotic Hawaii, land of grass skirts, swaying palm trees and aloha; patriotic Hawaii, soon to become the fiftieth state of the Union, a little bit of America flung towards Asia. Millions of Americans – a very small me included – were glued to the television each week to watch the variety programme presented by Arthur Godfrey, the aloha-shirt-wearing, ukelele-strumming, light entertainment impresario who often featured Hawaiian performers like Hali Loke and Don Ho. Another popular programme was the detective drama *Hawaiian Eye: Hawaii Five O* was probably just a glint in some television producer's eye. Americans were also eating Hawaiian: Hawaiian burgers, Hawaiian pizzas, Hawaiian cocktail snacks. Anything that could be garnished with tinned pineapple, was. Our neighbour Ted let us in to another side of Hawaiian life. An amiable man whose father was a good painter of cowboys and Indians, he was also High Chief Hululu, a proud descendant of the islands' deposed royal family. He gave me a copy of his family memoirs for my twelfth birthday – a reminder that Hawaii's road to statehood was not always paved with pineapple and alohas.

The first European to make landfall in Hawaii was Captain James Cook, the brilliant Yorkshire-born navigator. The islands were in political turmoil with rival chieftains jockeying for supremacy and things ended badly for their first tourist: Cook was murdered in an argument with the local people over a stolen boat. After Cook, the islands of Hawaii attracted a stream of European and American visitors: sitting in the middle of the Pacific they were a convenient stopping place on long ocean voyages. They also became a key port of call for the American whaling ships that began systematically sweeping the Pacific in the early nineteenth century. And American missionaries found them attractive too: they believed that Hawaiian souls were ready to be saved, especially as the native religion weakened after King Kamehameha II had broken the taboo against a man and woman eating together in public without incurring the wrath of the islands' gods. The kingdom rapidly became a colony of the United States in all but name and American entrepreneurs began to establish sugar cane plantations and cattle ranches. But the political situation disturbed these new entrepreneurs and amidst fears that the newly installed Queen Liliuokalani was attempting to introduce a more absolute monarchy, the colonists rebelled, seized power and declared the Republic of Hawaii. Sanford B. Dole was elected president in 1894. One day the islands were controlled by a native monarch and the next day they had fallen into the hands of a group of American businessmen – businessmen who soon realized that independence was not good for commerce. They pressed the United States government to annex Hawaii so that they could obtain big federal subsidies for exporting sugar to the mainland.

In 1898 the United States formally took over the government of the islands. At this point a canny East Coast restaurateur invented the Alohaburger – a hamburger topped with pineapple rings – to commemorate the further expansion of American dominion. Well no, not really. Because in 1898 no one really thought that Hawaii and pineapples had much to do with each other. Our modern identification of the islands with pineapples is the result of the plantation system, economic imperialism and insistent marketing and advertising.

The majestic size, unique appearance and edible flesh of the pineapple had made it a highly desirable botanic curiosity from the time that Columbus first encountered it on his second voyage to the West Indies in 1493. We know, for example, that Charles II dined on a pineapple with the French ambassador. As the seventeenth-century diarist John Evelyn wrote: 'Standing by His Majesty at dinner . . . there was that rare fruit called the King Pine growing in the Barbadoes and the West Indies; the first of them I have ever seen. His Majesty having cut it up, was pleased to give me a piece of his own plate to taste of.' Evelyn was unimpressed, compared it to quince and thought it was altogether too acidic. The king's gardener, John Rose, was determined to try and grow pineapples in England. John Tradescant the Younger, the eminent gardener and naturalist, had already tried and failed. Rose struggled with his plants, lovingly cultivating the tropical fruit in a charcoal-heated hothouse. He finally produced one and was immortalized for his great achievement: a splendid painting depicts him presenting the famous pineapple to the king. Following Rose's success, specimen pineapples were grown in the hothouses of stately homes around Britain. English gardeners must have been pleased to see the French failing to produce one until 1733: malicious rumours suggested that their inability to get to grips with the king of fruits stemmed from Louis XIV's attempt to eat a pineapple without peeling it. The fruit remained exotic and expensive.

Hawaii's early colonizers had realized that the islands, with their good soil, benign climate and lack of commercially significant native crops, were ripe for agricultural exploitation. Wild pineapples could be found there and in the 1850s the fruit was cultivated as a crop for the first time. Why pineapples? The nineteenth century was a time of tremendous expansion in popular taste. Huge population growths, the general rise in prosperity brought about by the Industrial Revolution and improvements in transport conspired to create a

Overleaf: The new plants that flooded into Europe from the Americas in the fifteenth and sixteenth centuries became objects of sophisticated appreciation and top gardeners strove to cultivate tropical products in European palace gardens. In 1675 John Rose presented the first pineapple grown in England to Charles II.

King Charles 2

demand for new and different food products in the industrialized nations. The increasingly affluent town dwellers of America, Britain, France and Germany wanted ever more variety in their diets. And pineapples – and other tropical products – provided just that.

Commercial growing of the fruit at first met with only limited success. Its potential markets were too far away and ripe pineapples could not stand the journey. Some growers began experimenting with the newly popular technique of canning but failed to make a go of it: the handmade cans were far too expensive and there was a punishing 35 per cent tariff on processed food that was shipped into America. The situation changed radically with annexation: the richest and most rapidly expanding market in the world was thrown open to the islands' farmers. Young Jim Dole – nephew of Hawaii's erstwhile president, now its first governor – entered the pineapple canning business hot on the heels of these significant political changes. 'After some experimentation,' he wrote, 'I concluded that the land was better adapted to pineapples than to peas, pigs or potatoes, and accordingly concentrated on that fruit.' The *Honolulu Advertiser* was unimpressed by the governor's nephew: his plan to can pineapple was 'a foolhardy venture which had been tried unsuccessfully before and was certain to fail again.' The prophets of doom were spectacularly wrong. By 1915 pineapples were Hawaii's second largest business.

Jim Dole's real genius was neither as a farmer nor as a canner, but as a creator of a market for his and other pineapple producers' products. He persuaded his competitors to co-operate with him in a series of generic advertising campaigns that promoted the virtues of Hawaiian pineapple, denigrated those grown in the West Indies and South-east Asia and used slightly fake imagery of Hawaii as a romantic tropical paradise in order to sell the fruit. Dole's aim was 'to make the word "Hawaiian" mean to pineapple what Havana meant to tobacco'. Pineapples took advantage of what a later generation of marketeers were to label 'associational values': eating pineapple was not just about canned fruit; it was about experiencing paradise. An advertisement suggesting that urban mothers treat their families to the delights of pineapple pie ('You don't know how good pie can be until you have tasted the incomparable flavour of the fully ripened fruit between layers of rich, brown, flaky pie crust') posed the pie against a backdrop of surfers riding the breakers at Waikiki beach. The pineapple's finest moment was probably 16 November 1916, 'Hawaiian Pineapple Day', when it was celebrated in the song 'Pineapple Rag': 'Talk about your Boston beans or hoe-cake from the South/ Or chicken a la Maryland that melts in your mouth/There's nothing in creation or that's in the eating line/That can compare in flavour to the "apple of the pine".' In the equally painful chorus, the singer wails, 'This pineapple, this pineapple, it's got me going right/I call for it at breakfast and cry for it at night.' Pineapples are perhaps not part of the recipe for domestic tranquillity.

Jim Dole transformed the pineapple from a relatively arcane tropical product into a thoroughly modern food, efficiently farmed on large plantations, hygienically packaged, widely distributed and relentlessly marketed. It, and other foods like it, are different from many of the other foodstuffs we have looked at because of the degree of human volition involved.

The political fact of colonization makes areas of land with good growing conditions available; colonial entrepreneurs choose the appropriate plants to grow; money is invested to convince consumers to buy and keep buying the 'new' agricultural product. It is a pattern we can see over and over again. And it is a far cry from the peasant slaughtering his pig and living for most of the year on salted pig, cured pig and sausages, not necessarily because he liked the meat but because it was all he had – and the pig-owner was one of the lucky ones. One of the consistent themes in any history of food must be our constant urge to move away from what we *had* to eat to what we wanted to eat.

Satisfaction of this gastronomic wanderlust can change the world as we saw

Overleaf: A *luau* or Polynesian feast is staged in Hawaii for the benefit of tourists. The imagery of the islands as palm-fringed tropical paradises of abundance was consistently exploited by plantation owners in their drive to persuade the world to eat Hawaiian-grown pineapples.

with spices, and as we shall see with perhaps the most controversial substance in the whole history of food: sugar.

Like salt, sugar is one of those foodstuffs we are inclined to take for granted. It is cheap; it is readily available; and – certainly in the most economically developed countries – we eat far too much of it. You can find sugar in cakes, candy bars and ketchup, loaves of bread and cans of peas. Along with salt it is one of the great Mr Fix-Its of the food world: if you don't like something add sugar. Mary Poppins was right – nanny always is – when she sang, 'Just a spoonful of sugar helps the medicine go down in the most delightful way.' And not just medicine. We are sometimes in danger of being overwhelmed by what Charles Lamb described as 'an interminable, tedious, sweetness'. But how powerful, how satisfying and how seductive that sweetness can be.

We are used to seeing our sugar white and highly refined but it is, of course, a natural product. Sugars occur in fruits (fructose), in milk (lactose) and most potently in sugar cane and sugar beet where it takes the form of sucrose. Its extraction from sugar beet is an interesting and exciting story.

In the early nineteenth century, when Napoleonic France, effectively blockaded by the British navy, was starved of sugar a chemist, Benjamin Delessert (a name tantalizingly close to dessert) developed a process for extracting sucrose efficiently from sugar beet.

On 2 January 1812 the triumphant inventor presented the emperor with a loaf of the sugar. Today, sugar beet production makes Europe the largest sugar producer in the world. But admirable as Delessert's ingenuity was, beet sugar is not our concern. The chemically identical but differently produced cane sugar, its production and the consequences of its production, are. For the moment it is enough to say that if beet sugar had been known to fifteenth-century Europe you would see few Afro-American faces on the streets of Chicago or New York and the Beatles could not have existed. You will soon see why.

Mankind has always had a taste for the sweet – a taste that was originally satisfied by the concentrated sugars found in dry or over-ripe fruits and almost certainly, at some stage, by the accidental discovery that honey was sweet if difficult to acquire. Rock paintings in Spain dating back to between 6000 and

7000 BC show it being gathered and the husband and wife team of Eric Valli and Diane Summers have seen it obtained by ancient means in the mountains of Nepal. In 1988 they described the work of honey hunter Mani Lal: 'With only a cord around his waist to secure him, he dangles over a 120 metre (395 foot) cliff on a rope ladder to harvest the sweet treasure of *Apis laboriosa*, the world's largest honey bee. Thousands of angry bees fill the air as he plunges a bamboo pole into the nest . . . Wielding his poles like giant chopsticks, he carves thick slabs of honeycomb into a bamboo basket lined with the skin of a wild goat. When full the basket will be lowered to companions at the base of the cliff.'

The dangers of depriving angry bees of their honey were outweighed by the desire for something sweet, but also gave a powerful impetus to domesticate the whole process. Beekeeping seems to have started in Egypt in about 2500 BC: the archaeologists Peter James and Nick Thorpe point out that bas-reliefs from the sun temple at Abu Ghorab depict a fairly sophisticated apicultural routine, tracing the progress of honey from hive to stone storage jars. 'The Egyptians offered enormous quantities of honey to their gods,' they write, 'one list from the reign of Rameses III (12th century BC) amounted to fifteen tons in 31 092 jars, probably a year's output from five thousand hives. Honey was also a very common ingredient in Egyptian medicines, presumably to make them easier to swallow.' Apiculture was practised intensively throughout the ancient world and the sweet flavour of honey often strayed into what we would think of as savoury dishes. But honey could not compete with the product of sugar cane.

Sugar cane may have originated in Polynesia, South-east Asia or around the Bay of Bengal. The sugar extracted from it was known to the classical world,

Overleaf: Honey is our most historic sweetener. The French photographer Eric Valli documented ancient methods of gathering it in Nepal where hunters daily risk death as they go about their business hundreds of metres above the ground, facing swarms of angry bees.

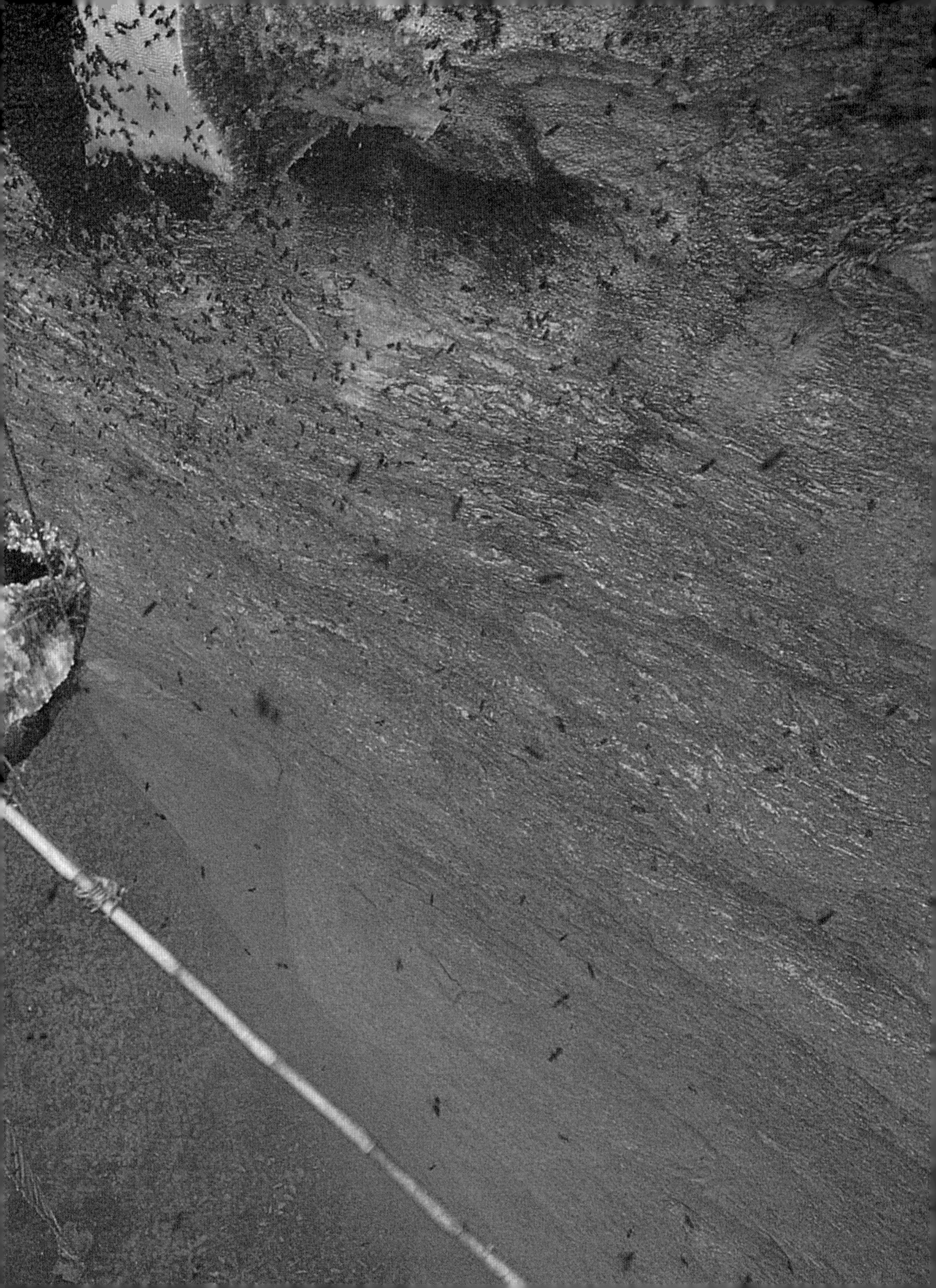

encountered by the followers of Alexander the Great when he invaded India and, of course, recorded by the indefatigably curious Pliny: 'It is a kind of honey which collects in reeds, white like gum and brittle to the teeth . . . it is used only as a medicine.' The Arabs began the cultivation of sugar cane on a large scale all around the Mediterranean and took it with them when they conquered new territories. By the early Middle Ages sugar was being produced from Syria to southern Spain and slowly began to infiltrate Christian Europe where, inevitably, the trade fell into Venetian hands. Sugar was a luxury item existing in the shadowland between a medicine and a spice, as likely to be found in an apothecary's cupboard as on a royal table. As Waverley Root tells us, 'In 1380 Charles V [the king of France who succeeded in reversing most of the English gains of the early stages of the Hundred Years War] was one of the few persons in the world to possess a fork; he used it to spear toasted cheese, over which in conformity with the current idea that sugar was a spice, he sprinkled sugar and cinnamon.'

The Iberians took over from the Arabs as the great proliferators of sugar: Portuguese and Spanish planters introduced it to their recently acquired Atlantic colonies of Madeira, the Azores and the Canaries where it flourished. Columbus experimented with planting sugar cane in the West Indies in 1494 and within a few years it was being grown commercially in Hispaniola (modern-day Haiti and the Dominican Republic) and Cuba. The Portuguese introduced it to their New World colony, Brazil, at about the same time. 'It was in the colonies of the New World that sugar really originated,' Brillat-Savarin tells us, 'the cane was imported there . . . and flourished. Attempts were made to use its sweet juices, and after a series of experiments syrup, crude sugar, molasses, and refined sugar were successively extracted from them. The cultivation of sugar has become an affair of prime importance; for it is a source of wealth not only to those who grow it, but also to those who process it, those who trade in its products, and those governments which tax it.'

As early as 1572 the writer Ortelius lamented that sugar which had once been found only in apothecary's shops had entered the everyday diet: 'People devour it out of gluttony . . . What used to be a medicine is nowadays eaten as a food.'

The great European sugar craze had begun: a craze which some commentators think still infects the post-industrialized world.

Sugar is a contentious and emotional food. Indeed, even calling it a food will rouse the ire of those who think it is nutritionally worthless and destructive to our general well-being. I shall quote first Henry Hobhouse, author of *Seeds of Change*, the incisive study of plants and history: 'Sugar, after the illegal drugs, and tobacco and alcohol, is the most damaging addictive substance consumed by rich, white mankind.' He points out that the victim of sugar addiction, 'becomes hooked on a constant flow of industrial sugar to the bloodstream and cuts down on fibre. The white sugar addict becomes liable to obesity, tooth problems and malnutrition, the last leads in extreme cases to the kind of "crowding out" which can cause vitamin and mineral deficiency problems and probably even cancer of the intestine.' Hobhouse links excessive sugar consumption to a variety of other evils ranging from alcoholism to a predilection for white bread. In the other camp, as it were, are Peter Bazalgette and Dr Tom Sanders, who while admitting that too much sugar causes tooth decay, assert that, 'There is no good evidence that sugar is harmful in the diet, and it does make food taste nice!'. All agree that sugar is a spectacularly concentrated source of food energy and that most people like it. Perhaps they like it – so much that they consume far too much of it – because it is as powerfully addictive as any drug or perhaps they like it just because 'it does make food taste nice'. Whatever the reason, the steady rise in the European demand for sugar created a product that has been morally tainted until relatively recently. Its production required labour, and that labour for various reasons was supplied by slaves. At least 10 million African men, women and children were imported into the New World to satisfy the demands of

Overleaf: The need to satisfy Europe's sweet tooth turned huge areas of tropical America into sugar cane plantations and the need for a labour force changed the world as African slaves were shipped across the Atlantic. These workers in Cuba share the arduous routine of their ancestors.

plantation agriculture. The fact that fellow humans were subjected to lives of captivity, suffering and degradation merely to gratify the taste for sugar on the table is a shameful episode. And the huge movement of Africans to the New World was one of the greatest population shifts in all of history. The beneficial end results of the slave trade are the rich ethnic diversity of the Americas and the development of a vibrant Afro-American culture in the United States which created among many other things the blues – without which there would be no modern pop music, no Elvis, no Beatles.

How did it happen? When the West Indies were settled by Europeans the demand for sugar was slowly rising and as Columbus' early experiment demonstrated the islands were suitable for growing sugar cane. Workers were inevitably in short supply. The dubious adventurers who colonized the islands were unlikely to be seeking lives of manual labour in the Caribbean sun; and the native Indian peoples who could easily have been enslaved were rather inconveniently dying off, largely from imported European diseases. A Spanish planter and future bishop, Bartolomé de Las Casas, devised a 'humane' solution to the labour problem. Why not, he suggested, import black slaves to spare the dwindling Indian population of the Caribbean any further suffering.

Las Casas' 'humane' idea led to the horrors of the Atlantic slave trade. Once it was established, he was one of the first to recant and indeed spent his last years campaigning against it. But Las Casas hardly invented the trade. Slaves had been imported into Spain from Africa as domestic and agricultural workers since the mid-fifteenth century: they were offered for sale in Seville's market from about 1450. And it was an ancient institution that had roused little moral indignation for many thousands of years. But the scale and intensity of the slavery created by the demands of the sugar cane plantation system, and later by the cotton-growing economy of the Southern United States, coupled with a change in the sensibilities of 'civilized' peoples, led to the moral indignation of the abolition movement which destroyed it 'forever'. 'Forever' is in inverted commas because slavery, both overt and covert, still exists to an uncomfortable extent in a number of countries. But most of the world has eventually agreed with the seventeenth-century philosopher John Locke that, 'Slavery is so vile and miserable a state of man and so directly opposite the generous temper and courage of our nation that it is hardly possible that an Englishman, much less a gentleman should plead for it.'

While slavery prospered so did the Dutch and Portuguese, Spanish and French, English and American slave traders who conducted the infernal business. But this is not a history of slavery or the slave trade. Most consumers in the sixteenth, seventeenth, eighteenth and part of the nineteenth centuries would have accepted slavery, however grudgingly, as part of the price to pay for the sugar on their tables. And, as many others have observed, as long as life for many 'free' labourers was brutal, uncomfortable, full of deprivation and subject to cruel and arbitrary authority, the abolition of slavery in the colonial plantations of the Americas was not a high priority.

European demand for sugar soared, but it began from a low base. As Braudel illustrates: 'In 1800 England consumed 150 000 tons of sugar annually almost fifteen times more than in 1700, and Lord Sheffield was right when he noted in 1783: "The consumption of sugar may increase considerably. It is scarcely known in half of Europe".' When I look at Jakob Vanderlint's famous figures comparing the food budgets of middling and labouring families in London in 1734, I am struck not so much by the fact that a middling family spent nearly one-seventh of their budget on tea and sugar, but by the fact that a labouring one spent nothing on sugar. Braudel gently reminds us that, in spite of a colossal growth in production and consumption, it was not for everyman until well into the nineteenth century. Sugar may have been slow to reach working class larders, but Henry Hobhouse produces some staggering figures for the hundred years between 1690 and 1790: 'Europe imported 12 million tons, which cost in all, about the same number of black lives.'

The business of growing sugar was cruel. It may also have been extremely unbusinesslike in spite of the vast fortunes made by planters, slavers and refiners. Many historians and economists have speculated that slave economies are lazy and inefficient. The easy money made by essentially exploitative strategies does not encourage long-term thinking or investment. One just has to look at the economy of the once prosperous Caribbean sugar islands today to see the result of such get-rich-quick policies. One of the eighteenth century's notable follies was the willingness of France to cede its share of Canada to Britain in exchange for being allowed to keep the sugar island of Guadaloupe. Canada today is about the eighth biggest economy in the world. And Guadaloupe? Well, it is a very agreeable place for a holiday. The so-called triangular trade which supported the plantation system – guns and cloth to Africa to buy slaves for the Indies to produce sugar and rum for Europe – was essentially a sterile and overly rigid use of economic resources. Colonial monocultures – the maintenance of non-self-sufficient colonies to produce one or two export crops – may have been good for the planters but they were bad for the colonial powers: it was often remarked that it took one province in Europe to feed a colony abroad. Waverley Root quotes from a letter that was written in 1647: 'Men are so intent upon planting sugar that they had rather buy foode at very deare rates than produce it by labour, so infinite is the profitt of sugar workes.'

Why did sugar consumption grow so rapidly in Europe? The most obvious answer is that once people got the taste for sugar they wanted more of it: what Hobhouse calls addiction and what we may say Bazalgette and Sanders call the 'nice taste factor'. And the Age of Sugar – 1550 to 1850 – was a time when the tastes of people of middling rank and above were increasingly adventurous. Braudel observes the introduction of new luxuries like tea and coffee, alcohol, chocolate and tobacco and notes how products from the Old World (cauliflowers, asparagus, spinach, artichokes and melons) were joined by foods from the New World (tomatoes, potatoes and maize) to transform European diets. For the first time since the fall of the Roman Empire novelty was becoming a prerequisite for good eating. It was very much the good fortune of the sugar planters and refiners that the increasingly popular products like tea, coffee and chocolate needed sugar.

No food arouses more feelings of guilt than chocolate. We worry about its 'addictive' powers yet enjoy the psycho-chemical effects that undeniably make us feel good when we eat it.

These three foodstuffs represent a new type of product. They are all mild stimulants that contain varying but significant amounts of caffeine, a drug which stimulates the nervous system. Although they may have had up-market origins (tea, for example, was legendarily invented in China by the emperor Shen Lung and chocolate was drunk by Aztec royalty) consumption of these particular foods became almost a badge of middle-class urban life. Peter Earle makes the point in *The Making of the English Middle Class*: 'I do not want to try to define what exactly is the essence of the middle-class existence. However it is impossible not to notice the vast number of vaguely middle-class things which . . . became common in the late seventeenth and early eighteenth centuries such as clocks, laudanum, fire insurance, street-lighting, novels, newspapers, tea-drinking and the three piece suit. Or how about eating too much sugar, statistics, economics, hobbies, clubs, the national debt . . .' Tea, coffee and chocolate were part of an emerging way of life.

For our purposes, chocolate is the most interesting of these new, non-alcoholic stimulants. Successive studies of eating patterns have regularly identified it as the most craved food. The American diet guru, Debra Waterhouse, recently made much of the statistic that 50 per cent of women would choose chocolate over sex as a pleasurable experience. This could mean that as a society we tend to over-rate sex and under-rate chocolate. But such statistics emphasize that chocolate is an especially powerful foodstuff. Writing in *The Biochemist*, Vic Cockcroft describes it as, 'a complex mixture of pharmacologically active substances'. We could describe it an interesting chemical cocktail of stimulants and mood enhancers. All pleasurable foods stimulate the brain to manufacture endorphins, often described as the brain's home-grown version of morphine, and these make us feel good. In addition to giving pleasure, chocolate contains phenyl ethyl amines (sometimes sensationally known as the 'love drug') which also improve our moods and other chemicals that affect the neurological mechanisms that deal with our emotions. Added to these potent chemicals are its oro-sensory qualities, among them the fact that chocolate melts in the mouth at a temperature just below our own 98.6°F.

Chocolate's ability to stimulate was discovered thousands of years ago. Allen Young, the great natural historian of cocoa, tells us that humans, like the rats, bats and monkeys that lived in the jungle with them, were first attracted to the sweet pulp of cocoa pods, but that the great breakthrough came when, 'Cacao seeds were mashed to make a crude, bitter tasting paste, mixed with water, chile peppers, vanilla and other spices, and maize to prepare a revered beverage'. It was this bitter, spicy cocoa that was drunk by the Aztec upper crust. Emperor Montezuma's *xoclatl* became our chocolate. (Contemporary Mexican cooking still contains reminders of how the Aztecs liked their chocolate. A popular dish, *mole poblano*, combines turkey with a bitter chocolate and chilli sauce.) Helped perhaps by its reputed aphrodisiacal qualities, the Aztec drink was enthusiastically received in sixteenth-century Europe although, in accordance with the increasing preference for sweet foods, sugar soon became a canonical ingredient for drinking chocolate. Cortés himself, the conqueror of Mexico, is generally credited with sweetening it. Following the usual pattern, the drink became a favourite in royal courts before filtering down to the growing mercantile and middle classes. The French and Spanish courts were particularly devoted to chocolate – its arrival in France may have been the result of dynastic marriages between the Spanish and French royal families – and Maria Theresa, the Spanish wife of Louis XIV, is reputed to have declared: 'Chocolate and the King are my only passions.'

Although we are accustomed to chocolate as confectionery, or as bars bought from vending machines or corner shops, it has been drunk rather than eaten for most of its history. And in England, where its manufacture since the mid-eighteenth century was increasingly dominated by a handful of Quaker families – the Cadburys, the Frys and the Rowntrees – one reason for the enthusiastic promotion of chocolate was the belief that this drink made an uplifting alternative to the over-consumption of gin and other cheap alcohols that were ruining the health of, to use a quaint contemporary phrase, 'the labouring poor'. The journey from Aztec love potion to Quaker temperance drink took less than 300 years.

For Ever Fresh

CHAPTER 8

Since the early 1880s, every male on my father's side of the family has been in the antiques business. The growth of the trade in America is just beginning to be studied, but most people agree that its greatest stimulation came from the World's Fair which was held in Philadelphia in 1876 to celebrate the centenary of American Independence. The fair displayed American progress – Alexander Graham Bell gave a series of public demonstrations of the newly invented telephone – and also stimulated interest in the past, encouraging collectors to look at American furniture, art and artefacts rather than collecting European objects. As a result, the trade in American antiques got a tremendous boost. Its early days were exciting as dealers scoured remote farms and villages looking for great examples of mostly eighteenth-century furniture. The business could be dangerous: one of my great-uncles and his carload of 'finds' was demolished when he arrived at an unguarded level crossing at the same time as a speeding locomotive. That was in 1913. My father followed in the family footsteps and was sometimes well rewarded: a particularly splendid Queen Anne highboy now in a major American museum was a chicken coop, converted by a New Hampshire farmer, when he came across it.

In the early 1920s he spent a particularly arduous winter antique-hunting in northern Maine. At one point he was snowed in for over two weeks in a tiny cabin near Fort Kent on the Canadian border. Fortunately, he had loaded the boot of his car with a case of Kennedy's Common Crackers, a useful if tasteless biscuit that could either be spread with butter or mashed up with milk and sugar, and a case of canned sardines – Maine was a big producer of sardines up until the 1950s. I often saw him eating Kennedy's Common Crackers, but he never touched a sardine for the rest of his life. 'I can't stand the sight of them, the smell of them or the thought of them,' he told me. So sardines canned according to a process which we shall see was invented for the Napoleonic era French navy fed a young antique dealer in the 1920s. Strange but not unusual. Once a foodstuff is developed it never really knows where it is going: the salt cod that was created to feed the pious of Mediterranean Europe became the staple food of African slaves toiling on Portuguese plantations in Brazil. Not only did the experience of his Maine winter put my father off sardines, it more or less put him off any canned food. I wonder if people like explorers and soldiers who have had to live on canned food for greater lengths of time also had an aversion to it.

Clifton Fadiman described cheese as milk's leap towards immortality; I think we could say that salting, canning, freezing and drying represent ways in which food in general has attempted to leap towards immortality, or at least transcend spoilage, climate, the seasons and other ways in which it is affected by time and geography. Preservation means that fish is always available on Fridays – as we have seen with salt cod – asparagus can be bought year round, even though they may not taste of much, and there is a freezer full of food when we are too busy to shop or too lazy to cook. Some preserved foods like canned peas have virtually driven the fresh product from our tables. Others like fish fingers have been invented from scratch.

Like the development of sugar from sugar beet, canning food, perhaps the most common way of preserving it, has its origins in the militarized conditions of life in Napoleonic France, a nation that the emperor's drive to dominate Europe had turned into a fortress and a garrison. Belligerent nations are especially interested in food. War, after all, requires energy – as Napoleon himself supposedly observed, an army marches on its stomach. And a navy also needs a full belly.

Nicholas Appert was born in about 1750 in the provincial French town of

Chalons sur Marne, was apocryphally employed corking bottles in his father's wine cellar and opened a confectioner's shop in Paris just before the Revolution. In the mid-1790s he began experimenting with food preservation using techniques that were well established for bottling and preserving fruit. He put the food into a well-corked bottle, heated the bottle in a water bath – which killed any lurking micro-organisms – cooled the bottle, added another seal and *voila*! Preserved food. Over the course of nearly ten years Appert was successful with fruit, vegetables, meat, fish, eggs and dairy products. In 1803 he submitted the results of his experiments to the French navy for sea trials: a government contract to supply preserved foods to the armed forces could richly reward his years of effort. The trials were a success.

An astonished naval officer reported that, 'the broth in bottles was good, the broth with boiled beef in another bottle very good as well, but a little weak; the beef itself was very edible. The beans and green peas, both with and without meat have all the freshness and flavour of freshly picked vegetables.' I am afraid I share the view of that historian of food preservation, Stuart Thorne, who writes: 'There must be some doubt as to whether the peas really had such freshness, but to mariners, used only to salt beef and biscuit, they must really have seemed quite miraculous.'

Feeding the growing navies of the eighteenth and early nineteenth centuries was a considerable strain on the resources and ingenuity of all governments. As N. A. M. Rodger wrote in *The Wooden World*: 'The happiness and health of the Navy were greatly dependent on its victualling, and yet of all the administrative difficulties of getting a fleet to sea, this was probably the most intractable. In order to feed men at sea food had to be preserved for months, often for years, but the best methods of preserving were expensive and unreliable.' Fleets put out to sea carrying vast quantities of pickled pork and beef, beer, dried cod, oatmeal and butter and cheese packed in casks. In 1760 alone the British navy bought more than 1000 *tons* of cheese. These supplies were augmented by barrels of sauerkraut – the vitamin C helped prevent scurvy, the debilitating disease that plagued navies – and by outlandish floating menageries. The decks of many warships were crowded with goats, geese, chickens, pigs and sheep brought on board to provide fresh meat. Naval diets were plentiful by the standards of the age but the quality of the food was a constant problem.

We can appreciate Appert's achievement all the more when we compare the French navy's opinion of his products with the British Admiralty's judgement on a contemporary effort at preserving meat in earthenware pots under a blanket of fat: 'In their appearance unsightly, and in their smell disgusting, unpleasant in their taste, sour and unpalatable, and in their flavour, whether the meat consisted of beef, pork or lamb, nearly similar.'

The more successful Appert went on to open a bottling factory and in 1810 received a government grant of 12 000 francs, 'as the preservation of animal and vegetable substances may be of the utmost utility in sea voyages, in hospitals and domestic economy'. In *The Art of Preserving all kinds of Animal and Vegetable Substances for Several Years*, published that same year, he claimed to have successfully preserved a dizzying array of foods: cherries, raspberries, mulberries, milk, cream, whey, chestnuts, truffles, mushrooms, artichokes, cauliflower, fillet of mutton, partridges and new-laid eggs. He also boasted that, 'As far as my knowledge extends, no author, either ancient or modern, has ever pointed out, or even led to the suspicion of the principle which is the basis of the method I propose.' Backed by this claim of complete success and total originality, Appert's book was widely published and his methods enthusiastically imitated. In England the firm of Donkin, Hall and Gamble preserved food in bottles as Appert had done and may have been among the very first to use 'tin' cans made out of tin-plated iron. These cans were a great step forward. Bottles were prone to explode during the preservation process and required rather more careful storage and handling. The biggest problem was opening the newfangled cans: axes had to be used on early examples. In 1819 the British explorer Sir William

Tomatoes can be preserved in a variety of ways and have become a feature of many international cuisines as a result. This shows thousands of tons of them outside a Mexican factory where they will be canned then shipped around the world.

Parry made the first of three attempts to find the Northwest Passage – the hypothetical northern sea route around the top of the Americas to the Pacific – fortified by cans of Donkin, Hall and Gamble's roasted veal. Two of them were opened and analysed in 1938 and, according to H. G. Muller, not only was there no spoilage but traces of vitamins B and D were still in the veal. However, canned food was hardly unalloyed good news for nineteenth-century explorers. Recent studies by Barry Ranford in Canada show that at least eleven of the 129 men who died on Sir John Franklin's ill-fated 1845 attempt to find the passage were victims of lead poisoning. Lead soldering was used to seal the expeditions tins of food and three years of dining off contaminated tins was enough to kill them.

Donkin, Hall and Gamble survived until they were swallowed up by Crosse and Blackwell. Appert's company flourished and survived into the twentieth century, but the inventor himself retired, and died a pauper at the age of ninety-one. In spite of his claim to be the godfather of the canning industry he was little honoured in his native France until 1955, when he was portrayed on a 12 franc postage stamp.

Early bottled and canned products seem to have been surprisingly good and well preserved. 'Surprisingly' because the scientific rationale behind the methods that were used was not discovered until much later in the nineteenth century by Louis Pasteur; so Appert and his rivals were largely working by intuition and observation.

Canning was relatively easy to perfect and rapidly became a cheap and reliable way to preserve food especially in conditions where, to use a military term, lines of supplies were stretched. Canned food was enormously popular with American pioneers travelling across the inhospitable Great Plains in the California Gold Rush of 1849. During the American Civil War it was widely issued to both Union and Confederate troops and swelled civilian demand for food preserved by this new method that made it portable, easy to store, almost immune to deterioration and comparatively palatable. Added to all these virtues, mass production was making what had hitherto been a luxuriously priced product affordably cheap.

By 1900 cans had assumed their modern form and, as Stuart Thorne points out, almost everything that is canned today, from asparagus to tomatoes via baked beans, peaches and salmon, was available then. Long before Andy Warhol turned a can of Campbell's soup into a pop art icon, the tin can was well on its way to becoming emblematic of industrial society.

The preservation of food sounds like a fairly straightforward process. Merely discomfort, starve or otherwise kill the micro-organisms that cause it to deteriorate. This can be done by making them almost die of thirst (preservation by dehydration), poisoning them with alcohol, salt, sugar or a substance like sulphur dioxide (chemical preservation), making life too hot for them (canning), making life too cold for them (freezing and refrigeration) or murdering them with lethal doses of radiation (what we now call irradiation). The least popular medium for preservation is alcohol, largely because it is expensive and imparts rather strong flavours – although, as Muller points out, brandy did an outstanding job preserving Lord Nelson's body on the voyage back to England after his death at Trafalgar. And irradiation has been greeted with an extreme lack of enthusiasm because of popular fears, which may or may not turn out to be well founded, that eating radiation-blasted avocados will make us grow two heads.

We have already seen how salt has been widely used as a preservative in foods like salt cod and sauerkraut, but the use of heat and cold must be the most widely used and acceptable methods of preservation.

Various methods of preservation and storage were already well known in ancient times. The Egyptians, as Peter James and Nick Thorpe tell us, developed effective methods of chilling: 'Egyptian tomb paintings show slaves fanning large storage jars. The jars were specially made from porous clay, so

Overleaf: Cans from one of Captain Robert Scott's polar expeditions bear witness to the role of preserved food in exploration. They have been indispensable items in every explorer's kit since Sir John Franklin's attempts to find the Northwest Passage in the early nineteenth century.

MOIR'S
TONGUE
HENRY
No

ATE & SONS Ltd
N & LIVERPOOL
1
ATE
SUGAR
14 LBS.
ATE & SONS
N & LIVERPOOL
ATE
SUGA
14 LBS.
2 PINTS
DUTCH CHEESE

that a small amount of the liquid inside would seep through and evaporate from the surface. Heat would escape with the evaporating liquid, lowering the temperature of the remainder, just as sweating reduced the temperature of the human body. The same method is used today by peasants throughout the East, and modern experiments show that the technique can cool water to as much as 77°F below the ambient room temperature.' We also know that the Roman demand for chilled drinks and puddings created a trade in snow which was brought down from the mountains of northern Italy. The philosopher, writer and tragedian Seneca – forced in retirement to commit suicide at the suggestion of his former pupil Nero – was disgusted by the habit of smart Roman youths 'not only sipping the snow but actually eating it and tossing bits into their glasses lest they become warm merely through the time taken in drinking'. Ice houses and pits for storing snow and ice were built not only in Rome but throughout the Middle East and China. According to James and Thorpe there may even be evidence for a Chinese ice house as early as 1100 BC.

Ice creams and sorbets, reputedly introduced from China by Marco Polo, were eaten in medieval and Renaissance Italy and spread from there into France and the rest of Europe.

Empirical observation showed that cold was an effective way to keep food fresh. The first woolly mammoth was found frozen in the ice of Siberia in 1799 with the contents of its last meal still well preserved and H. G. Muller tells how in the early nineteenth century William Buckland, an Oxford don, served his guests a meal of frozen mammoth and announced with a flourish, 'Dear friends, you have just eaten meat, one hundred thousand years old'. Muller also describes the market in frozen meat in Saint Petersburgh in 1800 where, 'the freezing was so rapid that snow hares were frozen in an attitude of flight, with ears pointed and legs outstretched. Frozen reindeer or mighty elk with hairy snout stretched upon the ground and antlers raised majestically into the air, disappeared piece by piece as saw or axe separated them for distribution amongst the customers.'

Using cold to preserve food remained the prerogative of the rich or an accident of climate until the development of mechanical refrigeration and freezers transformed chilled and frozen food from an élite fancy into a mass market convenience.

The first theoretical breakthrough in refrigeration came in 1782 with the work of William Cullen, a Scottish physician and chemist, who concluded, 'I suspected that water and perhaps other fluids, in evaporating, produce or, as the phrase is, generate some degree of cold.' So an eighteenth-century academic confirmed that what the Egyptians had been doing 2000 years earlier was scientifically sound. In 1834 the American inventor Jacob Perkins, who had failed to make his fortune with a design for a steam-powered machine gun, patented an invention that contained all the essential elements of modern refrigeration, the most important of which was the use of compression and expansion (an expanded gas will cool and therefore absorb heat). However, he was not able to make it a practical proposition.

In England in 1877 James and Henry Bell and William Coleman patented their refrigeration units and in Germany Karl von Linde developed a compressed gas refrigerator. Almost simultaneously two Frenchmen, Ferdinand Carre and Charles Tellier, were working on refrigerated transport. Tellier fitted out a ship, the *Frigorifique* (from the Latin *frigorificus* or cold-making and subsequently the French word for 'fridge'), which was loaded with meat and sent off to Buenos Aires. The carcasses of ten cows, a dozen sheep and two calves made the 105 day voyage in fine form. Carre did the same in the opposite direction, dispatching 80 tons of Argentine meat to Europe on the *Paraguay.* In May 1881 the frozen carcasses of 5000 New Zealand sheep were unloaded at the East India Docks in London and by the end of the decade Britain was importing 145 000 tons of meat a year from New Zealand.

We have seen in Chapter Two how the rising demand for beef was a major

Overleaf: New Zealand is famously home to more sheep than people – a result of the development of refrigerated transport which allowed the grasslands of Australasia and the New World to be stocked with animals to supply the nineteenth century's increasing desire for meat.

factor in the destruction of both the buffalo of the American Great Plains and the Plains Indian culture they helped to sustain. The ranching of the American West in the years after the Civil War transformed that sea of grass from a landscape populated by millions of wild buffalo to one populated by millions of steers. A new job, that of cowboy, came into being and the booming beef industry was largely financed by money pouring out of rich, industrial Great Britain. In *Beyond Beef*, Jeremy Rifkin cites some of the bigger British investments in the taming of the Wild West: the Prairie Cattle Company, capitalized for £200 000 (chairman: the Earl of Airlie), the Western American Cattle Company, capitalized for £220 000, and the Texas Land and Cattle company capitalized for £242 000 are just a few of many vehicles for British investment that were established in the 1880s.

The story was similar in Argentina and other newly exploited grasslands territories. All over the world British investors financed huge increases in cattle populations – it is not difficult to draw a parallel between the growth of cattle ranching and the development of the plantation system which produced Europe's sugar. Both fall into the category of what A. W. Crosby neatly tagged, 'biological imperialism'.

The Great Plains of America, the pampas of Argentina and southern South America, New Zealand and Australia were meat suppliers to the world and their grasslands became great cattle ranches that fed the slaughterhouses that filled the holds of refrigerated ships that transported beef to the workers and the city folk of the industrialized nations. The scale of business was awesome and influential. A young visitor to the abattoirs and meat-packing plants of Chicago was impressed by the relentless efficiency of the cattle-killing machine: years later Henry Ford used his memories as an inspiration for the assembly line method of manufacturing automobiles which transformed modern industry. The combination of technology, the nineteenth-century taste for beef and international speculation left us with a world cattle population of over one billion. Rifkin lists its alarming consequences: 'Cattle ranching is responsible for the destruction of much of the earth's remaining tropical rain forests. Cattle raising is particularly responsible for the rapid depletion of fresh water on the planet . . . Cattle are a chief source of organic pollution . . . Cattle are a growing source of global warming, and their increasing numbers now threaten the very chemical dynamics of the biosphere.' Even given Rifkin's self-proclaimed anti-beef stance, it is becoming ever more evident that there are too many cattle. And most people recognize that growing crops to feed cattle to feed people is not the most useful allocation of food resources.

But this was far in the future. Writing about the entrepreneurial years of the nineteenth century in *The Age of Empire*, E. J. Hobsbawm records that the major fact was 'the creation of a single global economy, progressively reaching into the most remote corners of the world, an increasingly dense web of economic transactions, communications and movements of goods, money and people.' A key part of this 'increasingly dense web' was the movement of food. Urbanization was the great fact of life in Britain, Germany, the United States, and France. The rich industrialized countries were becoming societies of city dwellers: in London the population grew from just under one million in 1801 to 4½ million in 1901. In Derby it increased from 11 000 in 1801 to 106 000 in 1901 and in Glasgow from 77 000 to 776 000 over the same period. Tens of millions of town dwellers were increasingly fed not by the products of their own countries but by food produced half-way around the world and shipped to them in refrigerated transport.

The new trade created considerable fortunes. An example is the Vestey family, billionaire butchers. Edmund and William Vestey were the sons of an affluent grocer in nineteenth-century Liverpool. On a trip to the sprawling Chicago stockyards William Vestey, then seventeen years old, noticed that

Overleaf: Cowboys roping steers were the romantic manifestation of a prosaic business: the need to raise and slaughter vast numbers of cattle to feed the growing urban populations that were a result of the Industrial Revolution. Far from being an independent spirit, the cowboy was an indispensable cog in the development of the modern food business.

large amounts of meat scraps were being thrown away. He realized they could be bought for next to nothing and transformed by canning into corned beef – a cheap, long-lived product that would give the cachet of beef-eating to those who could not afford the real thing.

From corned beef the Vesteys expanded into the burgeoning field of refrigerated transport and cold storage, the Internet of the Victorian and Edwardian food world. Just as the Internet flows information from where it is to where it is wanted, the refrigerated network made supplies of food more flexible – and more manipulatable – than ever before. In theory it enabled everything to be available all the time.

The Vesteys did not just ship beef from Argentina or lamb from New Zealand. As Philip Knightley describes in *The Rise and Fall of the House of Vestey* they also imported eggs from China: 'But shipping Chinese eggs in the shell had one remaining disadvantage: it was still a seasonal trade because the fierce Chinese winters slashed production. This made the baking industry a seasonal one also. Cakes like sponges and Swiss rolls were marketed only intermittently in those days . . . So the Vesteys began breaking the eggs in China, mixing them with a giant egg whisk, freezing the beaten egg in large tins and shipping this mix to Liverpool for sale to the catering trade. This simple step revolutionized the British baking business – for the first time it could bake "light" cakes all the year round – and was one of the factors of the growth of catering giants like Joe Lyons.' So the fact that impoverished Chinese peasant farmers could produce eggs more cheaply than their European counterparts, coupled with the ability of steam transport to carry those eggs economically and the new technology of cold to preserve them, meant that office workers could eat Swiss roll with their cups of tea in a London restaurant.

It soon became apparent that if cold was good, colder would be better and that lower temperatures and quicker freezing would allow foods to be preserved for even longer. Enter the nerdishly named but brilliantly observant Clarence Birdseye, known to his friends as 'Bob'. Birdseye was a city boy, born in Brooklyn in 1886. Brooklyn was an exciting place at the end of the nineteenth century. The recently opened bridge with its unsupported central span of nearly 490 metres (1600 feet) was an engineering wonder of the modern world that linked it to the dynamic growth of New York City which was already sprouting its first crop of skyscrapers. But the adventurous young Birdseye went north to the Canadian wilderness of Labrador to work as a fur trapper – some versions of the story make him either a naturalist or an engineer – and while there he began to appreciate and understand that intense cold was a powerful food preservative. His first experiments in the field were with fish and cabbage that he froze in temperatures as low as –50°F.

After his return to New York he began working on freezer technology and settled on a method in which the food to be preserved was pressed between refrigerated plates. Birdseye set up a fish-freezing business in New York which plunged into bankruptcy. In 1925 he tried again in the fishing port of Gloucester, Massachusetts, with the General Seafoods Company, which eventually became the giant General Foods. Birdseye froze fish successfully: his only problem was that he could not persuade people to buy it. In 1929 he sold out to another food company for $22 million: a lot of money to pay a man with a plate freezer and nearly a million kilograms (2 million pounds) of unsold frozen seafood.

The new owners split Birdseye's name in half to create the Birds Eye brand and applied considerable marketing muscle to their newly acquired product. They planned to launch frozen food to American consumers in the spring of 1930 and previewed the Birds Eye range in *Ladies Home Journal.* What was intended to be a bit of marketing fluff turned out to be extraordinarily prescient. Frozen food would completely change shopping, the magazine

Overleaf: Although bottling food is an old-fashioned way of preserving it compared to canning, refrigeration and freezing, jars of fruits, jams and pickles still give a cosy feel to a larder or store cupboard. In fact, bottles were the fore-runners of tin cans, first introduced in the early nineteenth century, that are now emblematic of modern society.

APRICOT
BUTTER
PICKLED
GREEN TOMATOES
APRICOT
EAU DE VIE
CRANBERRY
VODKA

GREEN TOMATOE CHUTNEY
ORANGE MARMALADE
PICKLED PEACHES
CRABAPPLE JELLY
APRICOT CONSERVE WITH ALMONDS
PICCALILLI

predicted, and create the store of the future, 'not a grocery store or a meat market or a fish market or a delicatessen, but all four rolled into one. It is a food store in the broadest sense of the word'. The Birds Eye range was launched during the first week of March 1930 – America had already plunged into the Great Depression – in the manufacturing city of Springfield, Massachusetts. 'For The First Time Anywhere!' a full page advertisement in the *Springfield Union* proclaimed, 'The most revolutionary idea in the history of food will be revealed in Springfield today.' The city's shoppers responded enthusiastically, but frozen food failed to make much of an impact on American consumers until World War II when supplies of fresh foods were interrupted. By the time Birds Eye celebrated its twenty-fifth anniversary in 1954, frozen food was being peddled in 200 000 stores in America alone.

The nineteenth century saw the exciting and vastly accelerated development of an international system of food production and distribution based on new technologies of preservation (canning, refrigeration and freezing) and transport (steam ships and the development of railways). We live with and indeed eat the legacy of those Victorian developments. We are accustomed to opening a can of peas or tomato soup. More of us than ever before eat frozen prepared dishes – thanks to the proliferation of the microwave oven, unforeseen even by the visionary Clarence Birdseye. And we live on foods that respect neither the seasons nor the bounds of geography. About one-eighth of the total production of the world's economies is made up of internationally traded foodstuffs that range from New Zealand lamb to Californian asparagus. This trade, as we know, is hardly new – the Romans started it – but the size and efficiency of the network that was created in our great-grandfathers' time has made it unlike anything that existed before.

Some people feel that this has contributed to the breakdown of what might be called the 'harmonious culture' of a time when folk ate wholesome locally grown foods, lived with the rhythm of the seasons and danced around the village green. I do not believe for a moment that it was ever like that for more than a tiny handful of people. As I have said before, food for many men and women, most of the time, was scanty, poor quality and downright boring. We will never really know what it tasted like but, without being overly whimsical, I agree with those who feel that although the great changes brought about by the Industrial Revolution were hugely beneficial to the health, hopes and longevity of the people who were towards the top of the ladder, they did debase popular taste by removing the bulk of the population from contact with real food. In *The Road to Wigan Pier* George Orwell describes the 'appalling' diet of a mining family in the 1930s – white bread-and-margarine, corned beef, sugared tea and potatoes. 'Would it not be better if they spent more money on wholesome things like oranges and wholemeal bread or if they even . . . saved on fuel and ate their carrots raw.' He concludes that it would, but adds, '. . . no ordinary human being is ever going to do such a thing. The ordinary human being would sooner starve than live on brown bread and raw carrots.'

Branded for Life

CHAPTER 9

In the summer of 1963 I was taken for a hamburger. Correction. In the summer of 1963 I was taken for a McDonald's. A radical new chain of hamburger restaurants – reputedly the most successful sellers of burgers in the world – had just begun to invade New England and my father, mother, brother and I were off to look at one. A gleaming new drive-in had been opened on the waterfront in Beverly, Massachusetts, just a few miles from home. The soon to be familiar McDonald's shibboleths were all in place: gleaming white and chrome surfaces, robotically friendly staff, hugely efficient ordering and delivery, limited menu, long stringy French fries and soaring golden arches interlaced to make a giant M. We perched on the chrome-trimmed hood of our big Buick eating our burgers and a sign overhead told us how many *million* burgers McDonald's had sold to date. This huge number, this inconceivable quantity of hamburgers was impressive. What did these millions of burgers look like? Would they stretch to New York, California or the moon? And how did they manage to sell so many hamburgers when they did not really compare in size or flavour with the burger you could get down the road at the Driftwood or up the coast at the Cape Anne Diner – or indeed at any one of 10 000 places across the United States where you sat at a counter and watched your order being cooked on a griddle hallowed by the grease of a generation's worth of burgers, hot dogs and sunny-side-ups? But it was quite clear from my first visit to McDonald's that the golden arches symbolized not so much a burger joint as a phenomenon.

The millions of burgers of my childhood has grown to many billions – enough, I can't help telling you, to circle the Earth 100 times. I say 'I can't help telling you,' because McDonald's brings on an attack of number-speak. It serves 13 000 customers a minute, owns nearly $5 billion dollars worth of real estate, employs 43 000 staff in Japan alone, has 15 200 restaurants in seventy-nine countries and a Lithuanian American coal miner called Philip Yazdik ate seventy-seven of its hamburgers in one sitting. These statistics are constantly revised as McDonald's racks up ever more mind-numbing records. The numbers are so high they cease to have any meaning: years ago the restaurants stopped displaying signboards showing how many million burgers had been sold to date – it was impossible to keep up. I am reminded of the observation of the nineteenth-century American physicist C. S. Pierce that, 'The universe ought to be presumed too vast to have any character'. The McDonald's universe may also be too vast to have any character. Certainly, when we confront it we are overwhelmed by quantity, by efficiency, by organization, by consistency and by a vast machine that in its home country employs more people than the steel industry. But we are not necessarily overwhelmed by the cooking. Nor are we meant to be: the company is not in the business of scaling gastronomic Everests. It is in the business of global catering and of selling something we have touched on briefly before: associational values.

In McDonald's case these are to do – on a large scale – with American culture, modernity and the market economy, hence its huge value as a status symbol among the young, the newly or emergingly liberated (its restaurant in Red Square, Moscow, was perhaps the most profound sign of the end of Soviet Communism) and people who are too busy to sit down to an 'old fashioned' meal. Associational values are the psychological, cultural and historical qualities we associate with a product. Sometimes they can be relatively simple. My two girls – three and five at the time I am writing – absolutely adore McDonald's largely because it gives them the opportunity to actually eat in the car and they are often given a plastic toy of some sort with their food. For my daughters, a trip to a McDonald's is associated with adventure and entertainment. Eating the burgers is almost incidental.

Associational values are increasingly important as a selling tool in our consumer age when there is so much that appeals to us. The trades of marketing, research and advertising have more and more influence on what we eat, and their practitioners are devoted to finding out why we like what we like, and applying those lessons to selling a whole range of products, including foods. In *The Hidden Persuaders*, the first book to examine the pervasive role of advertising and marketing, Vance Packard reported what happened when 'a psychiatrically oriented ad man' began to think of better ways to sell soup. 'Consider what the psychologist has to say about the symbolism of soup . . . Besides being a good food, stimulating to the appetite and easily assimilated into the bloodstream, soup is unconsciously associated with man's deepest need for nourishment and reassurance. It takes us back to our earliest sensations of warmth, protection, and feeding. Its deepest roots may lie in prenatal sensations of being surrounded by the amniotic fluid in our mother's womb . . . No wonder people like soup and prefer it hot and in large quantities. They associate it with the basic source of life, strength and well being.' And *you* thought people liked soup just because they liked it. It is all too easy to make fun of the psycho-babble employed in advertising and marketing but, as we have seen, food has always had tremendous meaning and symbolism. That meaning is sometimes overt, as in the eating of consecrated bread during Holy Communion. More often it is hidden beneath layers of forgetfulness or indifference, waiting to be unearthed by some enterprising marketeer or entrepreneur. What is unprecedented is the extent to which meaning or associational values, both real and engineered, have come to dominate the way those of us who live in the rich countries of the world buy and consume food. The concerns of previous centuries with production, discovery or preservation have been superseded by a preoccupation with manipulation. This is hardly

Overleaf: Creations of an automotive culture, roadside diners sprang up all across America offering cheap, fast food to a nation of travellers. Their now much-appreciated garish decoration was a vital way to attract the attention of blasé motorists.

66DINER

66
DINER
SOLD HERE
COLD
OPEN

surprising: economies of abundance are not worried about producing enough; they are worried about selling what they produce.

Before we return to hamburgers, I must stress that I am not being glib when I say we live in an economy of abundance. It is particularly distressing for anyone who enjoys food to observe that tens of millions of people – not just in Africa – are suffering and dying from starvation and malnutrition. Distressing because although we have the ability to feed the world, human beings are condemned to misery and death, not because of shortages or natural disasters but because of political folly and iniquity.

McDonald's was not the first company to sell hamburgers or even the first one to sell them cheaply. Nor was it the first chain restaurant. Its genius was to take one of America's national foods and peddle it with a cheerful and ruthless efficiency that was especially well suited to a society on the move. As Maxwell Boas and Steve Chain write in *Big Mac*, Ray Kroc, the long-term boss of McDonald's, 'could foresee the day when the assembly-line hamburger would embrace nothing less than a "System" – a patty to patron production line spanning a network of suppliers, truckers and outlets. He predicted that one day this "System" would cover the country, requiring specially-trained cadres of managers, assistant managers, crew personnel, field inspectors, regional and area supervisors: a crack corps in white shirts and crew hats to man thousands of stands from coast to coast . . . There is a science to making and serving a hamburger . . .' That 'science' as elucidated and formularized by Kroc led to the development of what we know as fast food, enjoyed by many but also strongly derided for its debasement of our taste and destruction of traditional habits like shared family meals eaten around a table.

Like all mass enterprises McDonald's and its profits thrived on standardization. It was able to sell the McDonald's meal to countries that had entirely different ideas about what food should look, smell and taste like. It seemed as if thousands of years of cultural preferences and taboos were being dismantled to make way for the golden arches. The myth of the global village, that we are all neighbours linked by an electronic web of entertainment and information and therefore less and less different from each other, seemed to be coming true and McDonald's was the chosen fuel. But its huge international expansion in the late 1970s and 1980s coincided with a rebirth of regional identity and a greater interest in asserting cultural differences. McDonald's, the authoritarian monolith, started to bend to local tastes and customs. In 1995, for example, the sacred formula for its bun was changed in Israel so that religious Jews could treat themselves to a Big Mac during the Passover when eating leavened bread is forbidden. Nevertheless, whether you are in Peking or Petaluma a Big Mac is a Big Mac. But the burger came before McDonald's.

Hamburg is a port and, as a member of the late medieval trading confederation known as the Hanseatic League, had strong commercial links with the ports of the Baltic Sea where sailors may first have tasted *bitok*, a Russian dish of grilled, minced beef patties. When Hamburgers – that is, people from Hamburg – emigrated to the United States in the early nineteenth century they brought with them their fondness for *bitoks*. These caught on with Americans and became known as Hamburger steaks. That is one theory. The hamburger could in fact have come from almost anywhere because minced meat features in a number of recipes in the Middle East and India as well as Russia. What elevated it to special status was the decision by some unknown innovator to put the grilled meat in a bun. Once again, this could have a number of sources. We conventionally ascribe the invention of the sandwich to the 4th Earl of Sandwich who wanted to eat something substantial without interrupting the important business of gambling, but it has many fathers beginning with the early medieval cooks who served pieces of meat on top of slabs of bread which functioned as edible crockery. Certainly, by the end of the nineteenth century hamburger sandwiches were widely popular in

Overleaf: McDonald's, the America-based burger pedlar to the world, has been seen as a symbol of progressive modern life in many countries. Its restaurant in Beijing in China was the largest hamburger joint on the planet when it opened and a culinary manifestation of Chairman Deng's aphorism, 'To get rich is glorious'.

McDonald's
McDonald's
McDonald's
麦香鱼

McDonald's
奶昔
CHANGE

America, particularly in the heavily industrial states of Ohio and Illinois. They must have made a cheap and filling meal on the run for factory workers, many of whom came from Germany, Hungary and Sweden – all countries whose people had a liking for cooked minced meat. How the hamburger made the leap from being a regional speciality popular with certain ethnic groups to one of America's totem foods is rather hazy, but it seems likely that it was first exposed to a national audience at the St Louis World's Fair in 1904, an event which was a major turning point in the history of food.

World fairs were a by-product of the Industrial Revolution and the developments in transport and communications that were associated with it. In Britain, Prince Albert was midwife to the Great Exhibition of 1851 which gave birth to the genre – and also gave the general public a chance to taste the then relatively newfangled canned foods. It was a dazzling blockbuster that mixed the products of industrial society with crowd-pleasing exotica from India and the Far East. Subsequent fairs and exhibitions were not only demonstrations of national economic prowess, they were also significant in the development of today's consumer society. They brought together goods from all over the world, like global department stores, and were among the first examples of how our world was shrinking. And, in the days before the mass media, they were a way of publicizing new products and inventions. World fairs were especially important in the United States where they helped to define and shape the national consciousness. The whole character of the population of the United States was transformed by great waves of immigration throughout the nineteenth century. Between 1860 and 1900 13½ million immigrants landed there and America changed from a relatively homogeneous society of mostly Protestant and mainly British ancestry to a patchwork of Irish, Italians, Jews, Germans, Poles, Swedes, Hungarians and many others who were united only in their appreciation of their adopted country's liberal attitudes and its promise of the good life. It was necessary to forge these disparate, polyglot immigrants into Americans. One way was by developing patriotic rituals based on the mythology of the founding fathers – Washington, Jefferson, *et al* – and the imagery of the stars and stripes. The pledge of allegiance to the flag and various codes relating to its display and treatment are typical late-nineteenth-century innovations. Another way was through the creation of a national cuisine. And this sprang into being almost fully formed at St Louis in 1904.

One hundred years earlier, in 1804, a cash-strapped Napoleon had approved the sale of all French territories around the Mississippi River to the United States government for $15 000 000. This deal, known as the Louisiana Purchase, was the single biggest territorial expansion in American history. To commemorate it and incidentally to show their civic pride, the city fathers of rich and expanding St Louis, Missouri, decided to hold a world fair, officially known as the Louisiana Purchase Exposition. (Under the vigorous leadership of Governor David R. Francis its planners also managed to get the third ever modern Olympic games staged in the city at the same time.) The fair occupied a huge site on the west side of St Louis, scattered with nearly 1600 buildings ranging from the most modest hut to 'palaces' of education and agriculture. There was a 79 metre (260 foot) high ferris wheel, a replica of an Alpine mountain, a statue of President Theodore Roosevelt carved out of butter and personal appearances by the once dreaded Apache warrior Geronimo. There were 10 000 American flags on display and new songs like 'Meet me in St Louis, Louie' were in the air. And there was food. 'The Pike', the mile-long central avenue of the fair, was lined with eighty food stalls. Among the stallholders was Ernest A. Hamwi, a recent immigrant from Syria, who was out to make his fortune selling waffles to the fair-goers. Inspired by the number of ice-cream vendors, he rolled up a waffle to make an edible holder for ice cream. The ice-cream cone was born. Or perhaps it happened that another immigrant, this time Abe Doumar from the Lebanon, suggested to Hamwi that just as pitta bread was rolled up to make a sandwich in Beirut so a waffle could be rolled up to hold ice cream in St Louis. Or maybe it was David Avayou, *another* immigrant, this time from Turkey, who came up with the idea. All historians of ice cream have their favourite progenitor of the cone. And even though ice cream historian Paul Dickson has pointed out that Italo Marchiony – yes, another immigrant, from Italy – had been making cones since 1896, everyone agrees that they made their mass market debut at St Louis.

The Middle Eastern origins of the three frontrunners for the honour are indeed interesting because of the parallel between the way a primitive ice-cream cone could be folded and a Middle Eastern sandwich rolled up. Unknown to any of the cone's modern creators was its 2000-year-old prototype: ancient Romans snacked on olives held in paper cones as they took their evening strolls. The ice-cream cone spread across America: Joseph Gustaitis reports that, 'by 1924 within two decades of the cone's introduction cone production had reached an estimated 245 million a year'.

Even more millions were touched by another food that was introduced to the masses at the fair: the hot dog, which had assumed its familiar form in St Louis. A long demolished house in the city was distinguished by a bronze plaque inscribed: 'There is a tradition that the wienerwurst was introduced to St Louis from here. A. L. Feuchtwanger, a St Louis sausage peddler in 1883, started the practice of selling a wiener in a split bun – popularly known throughout the United States as the "hot dog".' A wiener or wienerwurst is a skinny sausage, more properly called a frankfurter after its fifteenth-century birthplace. It came to America with German immigrants and was a popular snack food in the cities where they settled. St Louis, with its large German population, must have had any number of itinerant wienerwurst sellers. Feuchtwanger's gastronomic genius was to introduce the bun to the wiener. He supposedly used to lend gloves to his customers so that they could hold the hot sausages and noticed that rather a large number of the gloves were never returned. His brother-in-law, a baker, suggested a bun as a cheaper way of protecting customers' fingers. I am inclined to believe that this story is apocryphal. Writing in the *Saint Louis Post Dispatch*, Ellen Fuherman suggests that hot dogs were regularly on sale in New York City as early as 1871 where they were known as 'dachshund sausages'; and that the name 'hot

Ice cream attained mass market popularity around the turn of the century. The invention of the cone at the St Louis World's Fair in 1904 meant that ice cream could be eaten on the move making it ideal for restless societies – and children.

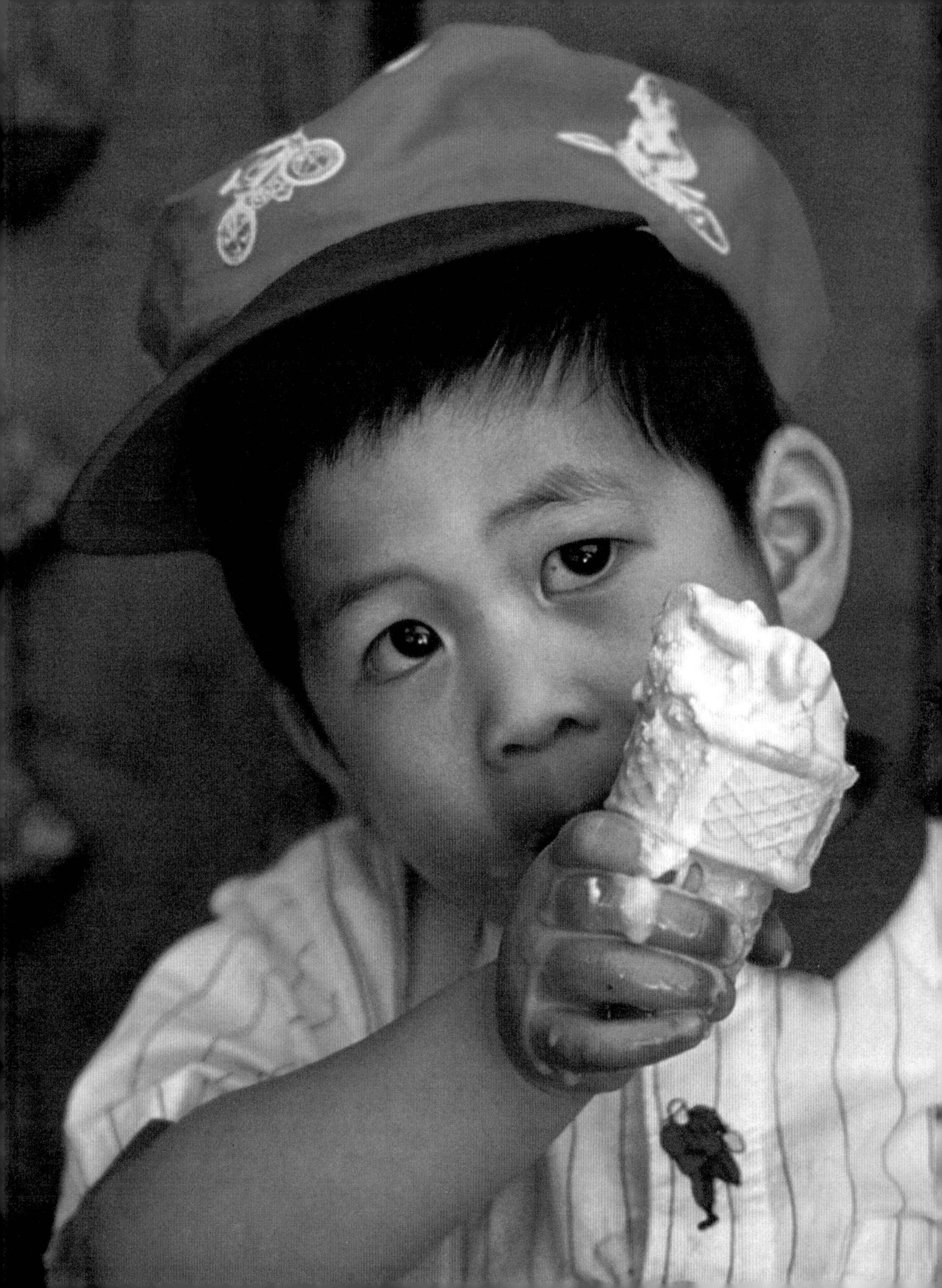

dog' was coined by sports cartoonist T. A. (Tad) Dorgan who was inspired by the cries of a man selling sausages at a New York polo game. Dorgan was sketching a cartoon of the vendor, whose cry was, 'Get your red hot dachshund sausages', but could not spell 'dachshund' and took the easy way out by calling the sausage in a bun a 'hot dog'. Another, less cheerful, story suggests that the term reflected consumer uncertainty over the actual content of the sausage – this was an era when there was shocking adulteration in the meat business. Whatever its origins – and there are many claimants – the hot dog made its nationwide debut in 1904. Adaptable and democratic, it rapidly became a hallmark of American identity. President Franklin D. Roosevelt treated George VI to an all-American banquet of hot dogs and beer in 1939; and the Americanized German film star Marlene Dietrich neatly managed to combine popularism with Hollywood luxury when she proclaimed that hot dogs and champagne were her favourite meal. Today, Americans eat about 37 million hot dogs a day.

Other innovations at the fair were iced tea, created when an exhibitor could not persuade visitors to drink hot tea in the heat of a Missouri summer, and frozen fruit juice in tin tubes. These were called fruit icicles and were the forefathers of ice lollies, known as popsicles in the United States.

The St Louis fair had attracted 19 694 855 visitors, put the city on the world map and firmly established the hot dog, the hamburger and the ice-cream cone as emblematic American dishes, new foods for a nation of new citizens. It was also emblematic of a new world. One of abundance and mass prosperity, of constant novelty and innovation. A world in which 20 million people would descend on an event in the search for new amusements, new tastes and new things to buy. The age of consumerism had arrived and with it the development of branding. Almost every foodstuff that we have discussed in the preceding chapters was produced anonymously and sold generically. You would, for example, buy sugar without being overly concerned about where it came from, who refined it or who sold it. You did not ask for a bag of Mr X's sugar or a pound of Y&Z butter. Two factors changed all that. The first was adulteration; the second was technology.

The late eighteenth and early nineteenth centuries saw the real beginning of mass production of foodstuffs and was a golden age for adulteration. Demand was high, expectations were low and there were almost no statutory requirements for hygiene or indeed integrity in the manufacture and sale of food. In *Food in History* Reay Tannahill runs through a catalogue of horrors, from Indian tea tinted with lead to bread baked with alum and pickles coloured with copper. The introduction of branded products was intended to give consumers products they could trust and names they could ask for, which would consequently generate more money for manufacturers to spend on promoting and marketing their brands in order to reach even more consumers and generate even more money. It is both a vicious and a virtuous circle.

The introduction of new technologies, especially canning, made it imperative to convince consumers that the foods produced by these methods were worth buying. This still applies today: every technological innovation in production or packaging must be heavily sold. Manufacturers say that advertising and marketing perform a service for buyers and create sales volumes that lead to economies of scale and hence lower unit costs and better value products. Hard line cultural critics see the process as being rather more insidious. Roland Barthes, for example, excoriated advertising for creating false values and inaccurate perceptions and for standing between the raw food and the finished product. He also felt that the advertising of industrially prepared foodstuffs dishonestly sought to create distinctions where there were none: 'By being faithful to a certain brand and by justifying this loyalty with a set of "natural" reasons, the consumer gives a diversity to products that are technically so identical that even the manufacturers cannot find any differences.'

David Ogilvy, one of the leading advertising men of the post-war period, agreed: 'I am astonished to find how many advertising men even among the new generation, believe that women can be persuaded by logic and argument to buy one brand in preference to another even when the two brands concerned are technically identical . . . the greater the similarity between products, the less part reason really plays in brand selection. There really isn't any significant

difference between the various brands of whisky or the various cigarettes or the various brands of beer. They are all about the same.'

If modern industrial production tends to make one tin of tomato soup taste very much like another, it is the role of advertising and marketing to make buyers appreciate whatever differences do exist. This is where the associational values which we have discussed before come into play. As Barthes sees it, food advertising takes one of three approaches: commemorative, anthropological or health. The commemorative approach links the buyer to history, culture and great events. Each frozen microwavable helping of chicken Kiev, for example, should encapsulate the glamour of the tsarist court. The anthropological approach emphasizes the feelings attached to food. Haagen Daz ice cream, a premium-priced brand, uses overtly sexual photography in its advertising both to highlight the sensuous eating qualities of extra-rich ice cream and to suggest, however implausibly, that buying it goes together with heightened sexual prowess and pleasure. Finally, the health approach proclaims that a product is good for us. As with ice cream and sex, the claims it makes can be far-fetched. The famous slogan that the high calorie, sugar-packed Mars Bar – however excellent it may be as a piece of confectionery – actually helps us to work, rest and play is a good example. Amazingly enough, we are often willing to believe uncritically what advertisers tell us. Barthes is almost beside himself with incredulity that we are sold coffee as a relaxing drink when we have known for hundreds of years that it is packed full of stimulants. Although George Orwell succinctly condemned advertising as 'the rattling of a stick inside a swill bucket' it is impossible to divorce either it or marketing, which includes the creation and development of brands, from mass production and the age of consumerism that mass production created. Certainly, all manufacturers would agree with Edgar Watson Howe's quip that, 'Doing business without

A favourite food of German immigrants, the hot dog has become America's national dish. Portable, classless and all-American by adoption (just like the people it sprang from), it is served at baseball parks and the White House.

advertising is like winking at a girl in the dark; you know what you are doing but nobody else does.'

The story of Heinz, one of our most familiar brands, is instructive. Henry John Heinz began selling pickled sauerkraut, grated horseradish (made to his mother's recipe) and celery sauce in the years immediately after the American Civil War. Uniquely, his products were packed into clear glass jars. The clarity of the glass suggested purity and careful preparation. It also had an extra sales bonus: recent immigrants to America who could not read the English on the labels could see the product. The business flourished throughout the late nineteenth century propelled by Heinz' endless concerns over publicity. Sitting on a New York City tram his attention drifted to an advertisement for twenty-one different styles of shoes. Heinz realized the power of a number in marketing, hit on the idea of '57', jumped off the tram and, 'began the work of laying out my advertising plans . . . within a week the sign of the green pickles with the 57 varieties was appearing in newspapers, on billboards, signboards and everywhere else I could find a place.' The first electric advertising display in New York proclaimed the virtues of Heinz through the use of 1200 incandescent bulbs, the iron pier at Atlantic City, New Jersey, one of East Coast America's biggest resorts, was topped with a 21 metre (70 foot) high Heinz 57 and Henry John toured the world selling his products: the first shop in London to stock them was Fortnum and Mason, grocers to the royal family. He never stopped thinking up ways to promote his brand. In Britain in the 1930s the company created the Red Army, an élite team of sales representatives dressed in dark suits and bowler hats and armed with tightly furled umbrellas – salesmen dolled up to look like guards officers in mufti. Among its key tasks was that of popularizing ketchup in Britain. 'We would whip out bottles of tomato sauce at every opportunity,' a Red Army veteran recalls. 'When we were having lunch in a café, we'd stand the bottle on the table – everyone would crowd around and ask what it was.' These stunts created a mystique for the brand that still sticks. I, for example, will swear that Heinz ketchup is better than other brands although I cannot possibly say why.

Everywhere we look in the late nineteenth and twentieth centuries we see brands built on the basis of inspired hucksterism. Thomas Lipton emigrated from Scotland to the United States at the age of fifteen. In America he harvested tobacco and drove trams before finding himself behind the counter of a grocer's shop. He had met his vocation. Lipton returned to Scotland and set up business in Glasgow. Like Heinz, he was a relentless self-promoter and keenly aware of public relations. He paraded the world's largest cheese through the streets of Glasgow in 1881 and, as it was Christmas, hid a small number of gold sovereigns in it. When the cheese arrived at his shop it sold out within two hours. Daringly, he dealt directly with producers, buying huge quantities of tea from plantations in Ceylon, for example, and selling it in Britain more cheaply than ever before. Middle-class tea suddenly became a working class drink.

The careers of Ray Kroc of McDonald's, Henry John Heinz, Thomas Lipton and others like Ben and Jerry, the hippy ice cream magnates, all expose a fundamental irony. In spite of the science involved in making and selling food products, and in spite of the allied pseudo-sciences of advertising, marketing and mass psychology, we still return to the 'great man' theory so popular in the nineteenth century and so definitively outmoded by trendier, societal-based methods of analysis. The great man theory says, quite simply, that history is made by individuals rather than by movements in society. The history of food shows how the actions of the few, and the sometimes conscious and sometimes unconscious needs and desires of the many, combine to create recipes for change. Who grew the first wheat, invented bread, or cooked the first chicken? We shall never know. Who ate the first oyster? 'He was a bold man,' said Jonathan Swift. A bold man, a hero or a fool?

Epilogue

Epilogue

There is a persistent fantasy – it certainly goes back well beyond my childhood – that in the future food as we know it will have been replaced. Technology worshipping kill-joys have been urging us to look forward to a time when eating will consist simply of popping a handful of pills which will provide us with all the vitamins, protein, fibre, etc. that we need. Gone will be the romance, the history, the adventure and sometimes the tragedy that surrounds everything we eat. These prognosticators have forgotten the elementary fact that food is more than just nutrition. 'You are what you eat' is not just a crude, physiological formula. It is a précis of the way in which what we eat reflects our beliefs, our culture, our history. Technology is unlikely to replace food just as it is unlikely to replace sex or literature or riding bicycles because someone has thought of a more modern or logical approach to any of these enjoyable, if cumbersome, activities. But it has changed, and will continue to profoundly change, what we eat and how we eat it.

Technology has certainly changed the amount of food we are able to produce. We touched on the paradox of hunger in a world of abundance in the last chapter. The problems of global hunger and malnutrition are not within the scope of this book, but anyone who is interested in food will also be incensed by the chronic problems with the world supply of foodstuffs. We *do* produce enough for everyone to eat. 'In both Europe and North America,' Nevern Scrinshaw writes in *World Nutritional Problems*, 'mountainous surpluses of food are produced with costly subsidies and stored at almost prohibitive cost. Moreover, Australia and Argentina have large quantities of grain and meat to export, and Brazil now competes for world soy markets. Thailand is a strong rice exporter, and a number of other developing countries have reduced or eliminated their need to import food and are potential food exporters. Nevertheless in the world today, more people suffer from malnutrition than ever before.' Like many other thoughtful students of the problem Scrinshaw wearily concludes: 'The true solution [to the world hunger problem] must be sought in a comprehensive process of social, economic, and political development that is ecologically sound and that directly attacks both rural and urban poverty. Science and technology have an essential role to play in this comprehensive process, but the final determinants of success will be political and social progress that leads to adequate food entitlements for all.'

While Scrinshaw and many others propose a political and social solution to the hunger problem some observers advocate a dietary one. There is no question that increased prosperity takes consumers higher and higher up the food chain and further away from basic foodstuffs. As Derek Ray proposes in *Appropriate Technology*, there are three main phases in the way food systems develop. As societies prosper there is an emphasis on increased production of foodstuffs and greater consumption of calories. 'In the second phase, consumers have enough purchasing power to look for variety: cereals replace roots, meats replace legumes and dairy products and fruit grow in importance in the diet and food system. Thirdly, higher incomes and industrialization lead to mass consumption with a proliferation of food products in the diet. This evolutionary path can be observed in Europe, North America, and most recently in the Far East.' We have watched something like this progress unfold throughout our story, from the simple wild grasses of the Middle East that were domesticated to provide the basis for the beginnings of the settled life to the novel, slickly marketed and eye-catchingly packaged foods of today. A dispassionate observer – if they could be such a thing – would see our economy of abundance as one of waste. Jeremy Rifkin tells us that by the time a 450 kilogram (1000 pound) steer is ready to be slaughtered it will have been fed on

1225 kilograms (2700 pounds) of grain. Who could possibly understand the logic of catching fish to turn into animal feed when as much as 45 kilograms (99 pounds) of fish is used to ultimately produce 500 grams (one pound) of rather tasteless chicken?

That may be an untypically extreme figure but it does highlight the sometimes rather peculiar methods by which we choose to feed ourselves. Remember the observation from George Orwell quoted in Chapter Eight: 'Would it not be better if they lived on wholesome things like oranges and wholemeal bread or if they even . . . saved on fuel and ate their carrots raw. Yes, it would, but the point is that no ordinary human being is ever going to do such a thing. The ordinary human being would sooner starve than live on brown bread and raw carrots.' Orwell takes the argument a step further, and makes a point that is germane to those of us who live in the rich countries of the world, when he writes, 'And the peculiar evil is this, that the less money you have, the less inclined you feel to spend it on wholesome food. A millionaire may enjoy breakfasting off orange juice and Ryvita biscuits, an unemployed man doesn't.' If you go to the remarkable Louis XV restaurant in Monte Carlo – its chef, Alain Ducasses, is widely regarded as one of the very best cooks in the world – you will see multimillionaires tucking into Mediterranean peasant food like risotto. And if you look around a supermarket you will see more average consumers buying mass-produced versions of dishes that Escoffier identified as the classics of French cuisine a hundred years ago. Like Orwell's Ryvita-munching millionaire the rich are rediscovering the basics. But as richer countries are, however slowly, moving in the direction of more carefully produced foods the poor of the world will be fed increasingly with the products

Overleaf: The Louis XV restaurant in Monte Carlo. Those of us who live in the world's richest countries enjoy an economy of abundance with access to dependable and ample food supplies. However, poor distribution and political folly mean that too many people on our planet are destined to eat badly or not at all.

of careless agriculture, husbandry and manufacture. High pesticide levels and poisoned fish are already a huge problem in the relatively affluent Far East. What is the food future of Africa?

The intelligent use of technology, coupled with a greater environmental awareness, will allow us to produce more and better food. Whether we choose to do so is an entirely different matter. We tend to find most food technology either vaguely sinister – irradiation of fruit and vegetables or the use of growth hormones in livestock – or wildly comical like the rumoured development of square tomatoes or turkeys with four drumsticks. But technology is an unruly beast and often produces unexpected results. I am writing this on a word processor, part of the information processing equipment that was meant to lead to the chaste and efficient paperless office. Today paper has reached dizzyingly high prices because the technology that was going to bring us the paperless future has led to more printed documents than ever before.

Consider the scenario at the start of this epilogue: all food will be superseded by pills. Now consider the reality. Like a growing number of scientists around the world Professor Peter Bramley of Royal Holloway College in Britain is involved in genetic engineering: he is tinkering with the genes of tomatoes to give them more of the qualities we desire. In America, Flavr Savr tomatoes which have been genetically engineered to ripen more slowly with the corollary promise of a longer shelf-life and better flavour are already in the shops. Professor Bramley's tomatoes are being developed to have an increased amount of carotenoids – antioxidants which some doctors think will help prevent cancer and counteract the effect of dangerous free radicals. So tomatoes with higher carotenoid levels will be better for us. The logical extension is that vitamin pills will not replace tomatoes; instead, genetically engineered tomatoes may be the pills of the future.

But if, as Max Beerbohm observed, 'There is always something rather absurd about the past', there is certainly much that is absurd about the future, especially when it arrives too early. The automation of food service is a good example of a future that failed to arrive either on time or as predicted. In about 215 BC the mathematician Hero of Alexandria invented a coin-operated machine for selling holy water in Egyptian temples. The idea did not catch on (neither did the steam engine, which Hero also invented). Modern vending machines offering drinks and confectionery first appeared in the late nineteenth century. In 1888, in a spectacular conjunction of private convenience and public squalor, Thomas Adams developed a chewing gum vending machine for installation in New York City subway stations. Ever since, used chewing gum has been a menace on railway platforms around the world. An outburst of enthusiasm for mechanization saw the invention of the automatic restaurant by the Horn and Hardart Baking company of Philadelphia: 'The man who walks into the automatic restaurant with the idea that he can sit down at a table and order what he likes from a waiter will be sadly mistaken. There are no waiters in the usually accepted sense of the term,' *Scientific American* reported. 'The two or three white-aproned men who nonchalantly roam around without apparently much to do are not here to serve meals but to remove empty dishes. You must serve yourself. You buy your portion of meat or soup, your glass of beer or wine, or your cup of coffee and you carry what you have bought to your table. If you are in a hurry, you may stand and eat, and enjoy what is popularly known as a "perpendicular meal".'

These 'Automats' survived well into the twentieth century. I remember that on my first visit to one on East 57th Street in New York I was amazingly impressed by the dazzling chrome walls of machinery with different pies, cakes, salads or main courses, each neatly displayed behind a tiny glass window next to its own coin slot. Put your dime or quarter into the slot, the door pops open and you get your treat – swiftly and silently. The first time I was tall enough to look through the back of the vending machine windows I was shocked to see teams of human workers toiling away behind the dazzling chrome. The

Overleaf: Soft drink machines in Kyoto in Japan foreshadow a world of automated mass marketing. But food is culture and, as long as we recognize that we are what we eat, the robotic future in which it is removed from nature and humanity may never arrive.

Drink
Coca-Cola
Fanta
AQUARIUS
つめた〜い
GEORGIA
Fanta
つめた〜い
つめた〜い
GEORGIA

Drink
Coca-Cola
つめた〜い
AQUARIUS
AQUARIUS
つめた〜い

robot restaurant of the future was a sham. The automat withered and died. But the 'perpendicular meal' survived. Japan, ever conscious of the cost of labour, has led the world in vending machine technology with over 4 million machines dispensing popcorn, pizzas, sake, sandwiches, cocktails, eggs, rice balls and pot noodles. So far Westerners, with their greater sense of privacy, prefer to do their automated eating from microwaves at home rather than machines in the workplace.

The vending machine capable of preparing freshly made dishes is only a few microchips away. Like the frozen eggs shipped around the world to make cakes for tearooms in Edwardian Britain, is it a sign of progress or merely change? For the first time in history we have the ability to control the destiny of our food supplies, yet much of what we do poisons either our earth or ourselves. We can eat what we like throughout the year, but what do we gain from out of season asparagus expensively jetted across the globe? And what joy do we get from the universal availability of the standard issue burgers and French fries if it means that families no longer sit down together to talk as well as eat. Food is a linchpin of civilization, to be enjoyed and cherished; whatever happens, we must not allow it to become less special to us than it has been to all who have gone before.

Bibliography

ALLEN, BRIGID, *Food: An Oxford Anthology*, Oxford University Press, 1994

BARTHES, ROLAND, *Mythologies*, Vintage 1993

BATAILLE, GEORGES, *The Accursed Share*, Zone Books, 1991

BLACK, MAGGIE, *The Medieval Cookbook*, British Museum Press, 1992

BOAS, MAXWELL and CHAIN, STEVE, *Big Mac*, Mentor, 1977

BRAUDEL, FERNAND, *The Mediterranean*, Collins, 1972

BRAUDEL, FERNAND, *The Structures of Everyday Life*, Collins, 1981

BRILLAT-SAVARIN, J.A., *The Philosopher in the Kitchen*, Penguin, 1970

BROWN, JUDITH M., *Gandhi*, Yale University Press, 1989

COADY, CHANTAL, *Chocolate*, Chronicle Books, 1993

COLUMBUS, CHRISTOPHER, *The Four Voyages*, Penguin, 1969

COOPER, JOHN, *Eat and Be Satisfied*, Jason Aronson, 1993

DE BENITEZ, ANA, *Pre-Hispanic Cooking*, Ediciones Euroamericanas, 1974

DEL CONTE, ANNA, *Gastronomy of Italy*, Bantam, 1987

EARLE, PETER, *The Making of the English Middle Class*, Methuen, 1989

FERNÁNDEZ-ARMESTO, FELIPE, *Columbus*, Oxford University Press, 1991

HALE, JOHN R., *The Civilisation of Europe in the Renaissance*, HarperCollins, 1993

HERODOTUS, *The Histories*, Penguin, 1971

HOBSBAWM, E.J., *The Age of Empire 1875–1914*, Weidenfeld and Nicolson, 1987; Abacus, 1994

HOBHOUSE, HENRY, *Seeds of Change*, Papermac, 1992

HOMER, *The Iliad*, Penguin, 1987

JAMES, PETER, and THORPE, NICK, *Ancient Inventions*, Michael O'Mara, 1995

KITTO, H.D.F., *The Greeks*, Pelican, 1951, 1991

KOLCHIN, PETER, *American Slavery*, Penguin, 1995

Larousse Gastronomique, Hamlyn, 1988

LE ROY LADURIE, EMMANUEL, *The Peasants of Languedoc*, University of Illinois Press, 1976

NEWMAN, LUCILE F. ed., *Hunger in History*, Blackwell, 1990

PACKARD, VANCE, *The Hidden Persuaders*, David McKay, 1957; Penguin, 1991

PARRY, J.H., *The Spanish Seaborne Empire*, University of California Press, 1990

PETERSON, T. SARAH, *Acquired Taste*, Cornell University Press, 1995

PLINY THE ELDER, *Natural History*, Penguin, 1991

RODGER, N.A.M., *The Wooden World*, Collins, 1986

SANDERS, TOM and BAZALGETTE, PETER, *The Food Revolution*, Bantam, 1991

SCHWARTZ, ODED, *In Search of Plenty*, Kyle Cathie, 1993

SMITH, ANDREW F., *The Tomato in America*, University of South Carolina Press, 1994

SPENCER, COLIN and CLIFTON, CLAIRE eds., *The Faber Book of Food*, Faber and Faber, 1994

STOBART, TOM, *The Cook's Encyclopaedia*, Papermac, 1982

SUETONIUS, *The Twelve Caesars*, Penguin, 1970

TANNAHILL, REAY, *Food in History*, Penguin, 1991

TOUSSAINT-SAMAT, MAGUELONNE, *History of Food*, Blackwell, 1992

VIRGIL, *The Eclogues*, Penguin, 1984

VIRGIL, *The Georgics*, Penguin, 1982

WATERHOUSE, DEBRA, *Why Women need Chocolate*, Vermilion, 1995

WEISBERGER, BERNARD, *Many People, One Nation*, Houghton Mifflin, 1987

YOUNG, ALLEN, *Chocolate Tree: Natural History of Cacao*, Smithsonian Institution, 1994

Index

Page numbers in *italic* refer to the illustrations